Reach Your Perfect Beach in and Around Naples Florida

Everything you didn't know you wanted to know about Collier
County Florida's 35 miles of beaches
Second Edition Illustrated with over 50 photographs and maps

By
Bernard Rath

REACH YOUR PERFECT BEACH IN AND AROUND NAPLES FLORIDA

Everything you didn't know you wanted to know about Collier County Florida's 35 miles of beaches

Second Edition Illustrated with over 50 photographs and maps

By
Bernard Rath

DEDICATION

To Art Ritas and Susan Calkins-Ritas who by virtue of their generous invitation to accompany them on their group pilgrimage to the Miami Book Fair rekindled my dormant interest in storytelling!

ACKNOWLEDGEMENTS

For their comments, corrections, suggestions, co-operation and encouragement I thank Jim Truluck, Sharon Truluck, David Upton, Lauren Rath, Vanessa Rath Menton, Jay Menton, Ray Morin, Ned Densmore, Ashlee Kelly, Elvira Lauer, Kevin McCaffrey, Art Ritas, Susan Calkins-Ritas, Drew Rath, Amanda Horton, Randi Jones, Neil Billig, Jenny Billig, Jay Giardina, Bertie Aye, David Albers, Susan Rath and Jeff Lytle

FOREWORD TO THE 2ND EDITION

From the winter of 2005 until the end of 2014, I worked as a driver of a seven passenger golf cart shuttle which they call a "tram" at Clam Pass Park in Naples Florida. During that time I'd estimate conservatively that over a quarter of a million passengers travelled on my cart to and from the beach. Among them were people from scores of states, dozens of countries and hundreds of cities. Since I am by nature inquisitive, arguably well read and a seasoned traveler with over a million air miles under my belt, many times my passengers carried on engaging conversations with me over the course of a single trip, or in three minute snatches over multiple ones. Sometimes we knew people and had visited places in common. At times some of the connections were uncanny. For example, a hotel guest from Australia knew a friend of mine from Canberra with whom I had been sailing in Sydney. On another occasion a guest from Calgary who was at a university conference at the hotel was an employee of one of my past company directors. Many of my passengers were inquisitive about a lot of things such as the flora and fauna of the mangrove estuary through which we drive and about Clam Pass Beach in particular and Naples' beaches in general. As a newcomer at the time, I didn't know much but resolved to learn more through research, reading, and multiple conversations with Conservancy of Southwest Florida volunteer guides and first-hand experience from walking in the parks and on the beaches themselves. The only legal way to explore Naples beaches is on foot or by kayak. So I first walked one mile and then two and then ten and somewhere along the way decided that I might as well see all of what there was to see. Over the intervening years, most of what I set out to do has been accomplished, by walking the entire length of the mainland beaches in addition to having logged many more miles on the island beaches.

There was a recurring theme throughout many conversations which ran something like this. "I have been coming to (or living in) Naples for 20 years and didn't know this place (meaning Clam Pass) existed". You can substitute any beach or destination for Clam Pass, but it seems that thousands of visitors and locals alike don't know what else is out there. They find a beach and of course it is indescribably beautiful and they go there repeatedly for the duration of their time in Naples whether measured in days, months, years or decades. They rarely explore alternatives perhaps because they don't want to risk a disappointment, are unaware of the options or just prefer what they already know on the assumption that it can't get any better than this.

The decision to write and publish this book came about because I wanted to share my discoveries, so that you and your family can enjoy what I have enjoyed. If you went to the Alps, would you be satisfied looking at just a single mountain? Would you return home and tell your friends that you went to the "Alp" on your vacation? The beaches in and around Naples Florida are special and forever metamorphosing (or morphing in today's internet inspired jargon).

They exist in this condition not accidentally but by design as a result of the attention paid and special care taken by prior generations of residents and visitors alike. They have succeeded with a spectacular result by preserving a balance between the beaches in their natural state and the demands of those who want to own their own piece of paradise.

Our illustrative maps are courtesy of Islandmapstore.com, a division of a Naples based marine consulting firm Turrell, Hall and Associates who have done much fine research and consulting work on the Clam Pass estuary. You are invited to visit their website and check out their enormous selection of maps of your next cruise, your last cruise or even your bucket list trip. Their placemat sized maps of all my "wannasee" islands are always close at hand. I hope that this book will help you explore as many beaches in and around Naples as your time here allows. We've added more specific travel directions in this edition, and an addendum short list of nearby places to eat, drink or just chill-out during your beach visit. As well, by request, we have added more than four dozen photographs to this edition. I am confident that you will ultimately reach your own perfect beach here in Collier County. When you leave nothing behind but your footprints in the sand, they'll disappear within hours and let those coming after you find their own perfect beach too.

TABLE OF CONTENTS

Introduction

Every person has a vision of what a perfect beach should look and feel like. As in the captivating lyrics of Blake Shelton's song each of us has a fantasy of "Some beach, somewhere" and like the sad protagonist in that song under many conditions most of us are happy to choose "Any beach, anywhere".

I have visited beaches all over the world and liked them all without exception. An incomplete list of my visits includes famous beaches like Bondi Beach in Australia, The Hamptons in Long Island New York, Seven Mile Beach in Grand Cayman, Prince Edward Island's spectacular and serene north and south shores respectively, Santa Monica and Venice in CA, and Manzanita in Oregon and Manzanillo in Mexico. Add to the list the Outer Banks of North Carolina and their magnificent sand dunes, the Jersey shore including Atlantic City, Wildwood and Cape May not to mention South Carolina's Strand down to the Isle of Palms or the Atlantic Coast of Florida from St. Augustine down to Miami Beach. And of course those numerous little Caribbean beaches such as Sapodilla Bay, Grace Bay and Long Bay in Turks and Caicos, Cane Bay in Tortola and my first exotic beach, Cable Beach in Nassau. In 2014 I visited one of the most perfect beaches I have ever seen at Conception Island in the Bahamas. Our sailboat was the only one there. From the quietest sandy cove between the biggest boulders in Virgin Gorda to the spit of brown sand at the base of the trash mountain that spews methane gas in Croton on Hudson NY where we anchored

Sainte Expedite, my Catalina sailboat, every beach has had its own special place in my memory.

Luckily for us beaches are not all alike ...some have white sand, some black sand, and in Hawaii the sand can be red or green as well. Many have sand packed hard enough on which to ride a bicycle or drive a car and some have sand so soft that it squeaks like especially cold snow when you walk on it. Still other beaches have craggy rocks interspersed throughout with sandy coves here and there and many beaches have no sand at all but as Carl Sagan might say "billions and billions" of pebbles. A beautiful beach may have driftwood, or no wood or a copse of dead trees or live mangroves. There can be a small beach on a cove on a tiny island that is more beautiful in its own way than famous strands that run for miles to the horizon and beyond and where the land is sold for a million dollars per linear foot of frontage. Some people think a beach is of no interest unless it is jam packed as far as the eye can see with glistening tanned skin covering hard bodies. Other people have their castaway moments where if they see another person somewhere, they feel the need to get up and move as the beach is too crowded or where a single footprint in the sand is one footprint too many.

Fortunately, fate and circumstance steered me to a quiet corner of the country, a place where the road runs out in the extreme southwestern tip of Florida called Collier County. The area's biggest city is Naples and has only about 20,000 people many of whom have done very well elsewhere and come here to relax and enjoy doing less of what they used to do and more of something different. In fact, Naples Municipal Airport has no scheduled airline service anymore but accommodates thousands of private planes and jets every year. Approximately 200 CEO's of the Fortune 500 companies own homes in the area, as do numerous celebrities, but for the most part the population emanates from the "heartland states" and most of the major wealth has been derived from what some might deem quiet and boring industries. The county derives its name from a Memphis born New York advertising executive, Barron Collier who escaped from New York to this section of the country in 1911. Over a few years he purchased 1.3 million acres of classic Florida swamp land, much of it under water, along with a few dozen islands and when he died in 1939 he still had the better part of a million acres left. While the city of Naples proper is quite compact with a relatively small population most of the western side of the county shares a group of Naples zip codes, so some 300,000 people actually can call Naples home. In addition, every year almost 1.5 million tourists visit and extend themselves out in a long pink line from Bonita Beach Road in the north to Marco Island in the south. As well, there is a special category of visitor, either affectionately or pejoratively known as "snowbirds" that visit for a month or three and swell the winter population by an additional 100,000 folks and then return to Minnesota, Illinois, Ohio, Michigan, New England, Indiana, Ontario or New York when the weather up there improves.

If you've read this far, it is likely that you are planning a visit and are curious as to what to expect or you already live here and are curious as to what you may be missing. We're attempting to cater to both groups of readers so from time to time one or the other of you will have to bear with me. Many of you will know absolutely nothing of what you are about to read. Many of you know some of it but not all of it. Judging by the people I have met on the Clam Pass Beach Tram there are a large number of readers in both camps. There are likely thousands of people who come to Clam Pass Beach and never even see Clam Pass, a mere quarter mile to the right when you arrive at the restaurant deck. To provide you with this first hand view and lay claim to being well enough qualified to write this book you should know that I have walked every mile of the mainland beaches in the county at least once and more likely twice. The longest single day walk was from Clam Pass to Wiggins Pass and back in the same gorgeous day, a distance of about ten miles which isn't recommended without some shorter warm up walks first. The island beaches in the county have been more of a challenge because the wind, weather and tides often dictate where one can go and the duration of the stay while the walk often comes at the end of a kayak paddle and later the return paddle always looms. The longest single day walk on Keewaydin Island was 6.2 miles round-trip followed by a long paddle back to the car. It may take a few more editions but at some point I intend to make the claim to have walked all of the navigable portions of the island beaches as well.

We are going to start our tour in the far northern reaches of Collier County in a preserve and park called Barefoot Beach and work our way south to Morgan Beach at the tip of Cape Romano. Though this is not a hiking guide, there is much information of value to beach walkers and if you want to see some of these sights you are going to have to walk since all other methods of travel are restricted. While it may not be unique to Collier, walking is the only method of transportation that is allowed on this county's beaches. If you don't want to walk the beach that's fine, you may just set your butt down anywhere you want. You likely won't see a lot of stuff that is being referenced but at least you will have read about it. In fact there is a very reputable genre of travel literature called "armchair travel" especially for people who are never actually going to visit the Amazon or Patagonia or the Galapagos, so if you are going to be one of those people who goes to Clam Pass Park and never gets to Clam Pass, so be it. At least you'll know it's there and know a little something about it and together we will have coined a phrase for a new genre of travel literature. We can call it "tablet travel" as you supplement the interests that have been inspired by this book and its photographs with graphics and images from the internet via You Tube, Google Earth, Google Images or Wikipedia.

Map Image provided by IslandMapstore.com, Copyright 2011 © Turrell, Hall and Associates

Barefoot Beach Park and Preserve

Directions

- Drive north from Naples to Bonita Beach Rd. on either Route 41 (Tamiami Trail) or I75. The exit from I75 is #116.
- Then drive west (left turn coming from the south) and watch for left turn just before Coconut Jack's Bar
- Go slowly through the "Dragon Tower. Don't forget to wave."
- Drive slowly along the red brick road until pavement starts again.

Parking	🌴🌴🌴🌴🌴
Food, Drink, Amenities	🌴🌴🌴🌴
Toilets/Change Rooms/Showers	🌴🌴🌴🌴
Rentals	🌴🌴🌴🌴🌴
Shelling	🌴🌴🌴🌴🌴
Proximity and variety of off-site amenities	🌴

In 2014, Barefoot Beach was ranked the second best beach in the USA, by Dr. Beach, the "nom de plume" for a Florida International University (FIU) professor named Dr. Stephen P. Leatherman. That's saying a lot as the competition includes all of the Atlantic and Pacific seaboards, as well as Hawaii. The methodology of the choice is a tiny bit suspect as once a beach has been ranked Number 1, it is retired from the competition, thus providing a chance for other beaches further down the rankings an ultimate opportunity at their own "day in the sun". Nonetheless, this is a terrific beach by any standard and Dr. Beach has fifty standards that you can find delineated on his website. Just do a Google search for "drbeach", if you want to find out more. The park beach itself runs for 8,000 linear feet, yet the whole of this section of sand runs an additional 5 miles north into the next county before ending at another inlet. Thus if you are adventurous and northbound you can just keep on walking. The south end of it dead ends at Wiggins Pass and the north end brings you to Little Hickory Island, Doc's Beach House and perhaps a different book as you've entered Lee County.

If you are driving to Barefoot Beach, you literally have to leave Collier County to get there. It's quite similar to Point Roberts, Washington in that the only way to get to it by land is to leave the USA, enter Canada and then re-enter the USA at Point Roberts. This spot is eerily similar as there are also two different guard kiosks with two different sets of officials to monitor your progress as you unwittingly crisscross a maze of jurisdictional territories that includes at least two counties and an HOA (Homeowners' Association). The first guard who works for the real estate owners' association appears in an edifice that rivals the Torugart Pass gate between China and Kyrgyzstan but unlike their pistol packing alter egos these guards only function is to wave you through to the next checkpoint.

Barefoot Beach is easy to find and yet many can't find it, likely because it is deceptively difficult to enter. There are a number of easy alternatives further to the south including the enticing and easily entered cavernous garage with electronic space availability displays, just a few miles away at Vanderbilt Beach. Many Collier residents and visitors choose to skip this one as they appear to be thrown off the scent of the public beach by the private security guard and imposing station. That may have been by design and a preferred outcome for the well heeled property owners within, but you are strongly urged to persevere to visit Barefoot Beach. A large number of visitors to this park are residents or vacationers from Lee County. Bonita Springs and the new village of Estero who have very limited parking at their own public beach access points. Many of these people buy annual parking passes to Barefoot Beach, which by the way are less expensive than the Lee County ones, though the latter also include boat ramp access. The area has a large parking lot with 356 parking spaces which is good news and bad news. The good news of course is that you likely will be able to find a parking space on most days. The bad news is that so are seven or eight hundred other people during the busiest of days each year from Presidents' Day through Easter week-end.

Getting there is not that hard. It is the westbound Exit 116 on I75 or you can drive north on Tamiami Trail (Rte. 41) from anywhere else in Collier County. Follow Bonita Beach Road and in about one and a half miles west from Tamiami Trail look for Coconut Jack's waterfront restaurant. Just before that, you will see a sign on the right side of the road that alerts you to turn left for the park at the next opportunity into what appears to be a housing development, which it is. It is called Lely Barefoot Beach. There you will see that most imposing two story guard shack. The upper level seems somewhat superfluous, though I suppose it is a good place from which to drop the boiling oil should the barbarians at the gate become unruly. I looked for the archery slots as I went by the other day and didn't see any so that might have been an opportunity missed by the HOA to get the most out of that second story. If you were driving west toward the water and the road suddenly turns sharply to the right and you find that you are headed north then you missed the turn. Turn around and go back south to make the right turn this time, just after Doc's Beach House.

Once you get off the main road, you'll need to make a choice. If it is the off season and you have a Collier County beach parking pass and just want to hang out and drink a cold beer give the guard a wave and hang a hard right before the two story shack (can we call it by its rightful name?....the Dragon

Tower). There are 136 parking spaces within Collier County right there on the Lee County border, though in season, finding a space in this small lot is very difficult. Like Point Roberts, you can park the car, walk over the border and legally drink a beverage with alcoholic content within sight of beach sand.

After you park, walk in a northwesterly direction for a few yards, pull an Alice in Wonderland and go through the hole in the hedge and lo and behold you are back in Lee County. Head for Doc's Beach House and choose from a wide selection of ice-cold beer and soda pop that sweats when you take it out of the large galvanized metal tub from a bygone era. You can figure out the rest later....or not. Your day might just begin and end right here. As it is just north of the county line this is also the closest place to rent personal watercraft (i.e. Jet Ski's) or go parasailing. There is a perfect view of the sunset and they serve Chicago style pizza. We are not judgmental and you are not required to walk on the beach to enjoy this book. Periodically you can choose to sit on it, beside it or in front of it. Circumstances change. Life requires adaptation. There aren't many publicly accessible places like Doc's Beach House on any of Collier County's main beaches, which is likely partly by design of the residents and partly the high price of beach front real estate these days. Doc's has been around since 1987 and things were different then. There was a similar one until recently, the old Vanderbilt Inn at the foot of 111th Ave. N in Naples, but it was razed to make way for multi-million dollar condominiums. There is more to read on that in the section on Vanderbilt Beach.

If you do want to go to Barefoot Beach Preserve Park then I am afraid there is no way around it. You are going to have to pass by the Dragon Tower. After you have made the left turn from Bonita Beach Road and assuming you have decided to bypass the hole in the hedge to Doc's Beach House to the west, then just go straight past the Dragon Tower. Unlike most people standing in housing community guard shacks and refusing entry to non-residents, this poor individual has no such charge. While employed by the owners of multi-million dollar beach houses to maintain the face of a gated community, the actual charge is to let all the commoners in so that they can go to the park which is south of his community and just be their common selves. Out of deference to the owners of all these rarely occupied, multi-storied, multi-million dollar beach shacks, I follow all the signs and respect the 20 mph speed limit. My theory is that the speed limits are set so low, the bricks in the cobblestone road set so unevenly and the frequent speed bumps annoyingly jarring, to remind you that you are in the presence of privilege and that your presence while tolerated is temporary. I am ever so glad to be back in Collier County again, when the road turns back to macadam and we see our friendly Collier County parking attendant practicing his golf swing outside of his clapboard shack with the outhouse in the back.

Barefoot Beach Park is officially a preserve as well. At 342 acres it is one of the last mostly undeveloped barrier islands in this section of Florida and home to a sizeable colony of Gopher Tortoises. While both Clam Pass Park and Delnor

Wiggins Park have a few of these, Barefoot Beach Preserve is literally crawling with them. Signs urge you to check under the car before driving away, as the tortoises like to hang in the shade under your car while you are out frying in the sun. Unlike turtles that live in water, tortoises live on land. I know that is an oversimplification that some will take issue with, but it works for our purposes. On more than one occasion, I have had to rescue a tortoise from the hands of a well meaning northern visitor about to toss it into the water from whence it did not come, on the grounds that the "turtle" was lost and looked dried out. Trust me, if you lived on the beach for fifty years, you'd look dried out too. I also had to rescue a kidnapped tortoise from the arms of a college student who wanted to take it home as a pet. I empathized with his need since my son's fraternity had a pet pig named Ripley living among them. There is no better way to impress sorority girls than to show them your exotic pets and I am sure the tortoise would have lived a long, happy, though somewhat besotted life at an institute of higher learning. While saving the gopher tortoise was neat it wasn't nearly as satisfying as sending the kid at the Clam Pass parking lot with a four foot juvenile alligator under his beach blanket back to the pond to release it. I am still not sure what he was thinking but I doubt that the sorority girls would have been impressed with this particular choice of pet.

Gopher tortoises live in burrows in the sand dunes behind the beach which is presumably why they acquired this descriptive moniker. The burrows can be up to 10 feet deep and more than 40 feet long. While not officially listed as endangered they are protected and officially considered "threatened" and can live to sixty years of age. These guys can be a problem for builders and developers but unlike the burrowing owls in the classic Carl Hiaasen book "Hoot" their existence doesn't stop development, just delays it. Once they are rounded up, appropriate mitigation fees paid to the interested parties and then resettled in a gopher tortoise habitat in some less expensive part of the community usually way inland, then the development can proceed. People make money from swapping these mitigation credits and it seems to me there is likely no better tenant anywhere than one which lives in the dirt, eats weeds, rarely drinks, has a rich relation to pay the rent and doesn't talk back.

If you've got the right stuff and forced yourself to run the Dragon Tower gauntlet, you likely have the right stuff in you to walk to the southern end of the beach. I recommend bypassing the first few parking lots and parking in the last most southerly lot. It's easy enough to find as it is a dead-end. This isn't strictly necessary, but will reduce your need to walk a significantly greater distance. At the southern end of this walk you will have arrived at the northern side of Wiggins Pass. The one way distance is less than a mile and you can do the round trip in about 45 minutes depending on how much time you spend frittering, shelling or deciphering flotsam and jetsam. As a result of this beach being a preserve as well as a park, there are no buildings of any sort on your left as walk south. As you read further in this book, it will become apparent to you that I prefer beaches without buildings and islands without bridges. That's just me so don't let it influence your opinion of a particular beach unduly. There is a goodly number of dead trees along this stretch at the end and walking among and between them can present a navigation challenge at high tide. There is also often a tall scarp (a vertical wall of sand, roots and dirt) that will further limit your range to the east. In November 2012, this scarp was five feet high. Consequently, you should take this walk at mean low tide or an hour or two before. Don't head down to the southernmost point of this beach at the end of an outbound tide, hang out there for a couple of hours and then expect to be able to walk back unimpeded. It's not a life or death thing but it means you will have to wait around for a while until you can wade around the deadfall. There is a cool, free I-Phone app called Shralp Tide that does an amazing job for any place in the world that I recommend you download. Many visitors from landlocked places are not completely familiar with tide cycles, having frequented freshwater beaches for most of their lives. Even those from maritime states can become confused when they come to Collier County because generally there are four tides in a cycle rather than two. For the most part, there is a high and low tide every six hours on Collier's beaches with one set of highs and lows being more extreme than the other. While the average amplitude of each tide varies, figure an average of from 2 to 3 feet and anything more or less as a bonus surprise during a full moon phase. The Shralp tide app I mentioned takes care of all of that for you, and when you turn the phone horizontally it will graph where you are on the cycle.

Wiggins Pass is a major recreational boating inlet. While it doesn't have the high volume traffic of Gordon Pass, it has a lot of it nevertheless. Swimming is prohibited by law, but even if weren't, it is just plain dumb to swim here as the tidal currents and eddies can be strong and unpredictable and even if you master those the odds are you going to get whacked by a passing boat. The pass is actually the mouth of the Cocohatchee River, which in addition to giving Gulf access to thousands of boat owners who live in its watershed, drains an area of more than 3,000 acres to the north and east. There is also a public boat ramp operated by Collier County Parks and Recreation nearby and even a great many Bonita Springs residents and Lee County private marinas use this outlet to get to open water. Compared to the great lighthouses of fact and fiction, the light at Wiggins Pass is a major disappointment but it does work and I am sure many a weary gulf wanderer has welcomed it. The dredging of Wiggins Pass is a regular bone of local political contention every few years. Just as "One man's junk is another man's treasure", I find that often the "beach walker's shoal is a boater's nightmare". The wind, waves, tides and weather in this area give us an ever changing landscape to explore, much to the chagrin of the local boaters. You can visit this area often and be impressed by its constant metamorphoses

If you choose to visit Barefoot Beach and plunk your butt in the sand then park in the first parking section you come to once you enter the park. There is a nice snack bar and rental concession here, good bathrooms and a canoe/kayak launch site. The Collier County Parks and Recreation Department together with the Friends of Barefoot Beach volunteer organization runs various interpretive wildlife programs here, (see the latter's site for a current schedule) and there is a well marked nature trail to hike. Additionally, there is an easy one and a half mile long, well marked canoe/kayak trail, where for a small fee you can pre-register to take a canoe trip with a park ranger or launch for free when you bring your own non-motorized vessel. This beach usually has good shelling the further you travel south from the parking lots. There is also a great website for "friends of barefoot beach" with lots of information on nature tours and where Sharon Truluck (who along with her husband Jim also conduct Clam Pass tours in season) writes a blog on the flora and fauna to be found here.

The county line "hole in the hedge"   You are looking
north into Lee County and Doc's Beach house and the Jet
Ski rentals are just beyond that group of cars. The hedge
is comprised of Sea grape plants.

Author and scarp in perspective at Barefoot Beach. This is either a short man and a tall scarp, or a short scarp and a tall man or a Hobbit out for a few rays.

That's a lotta scarp!

Barefoot Beach view to the north from Wiggins Pass

Barefoot Beach view to the south towards Wiggins Pass

View at the south end of Barefoot Beach to Delnor
Wiggins Park across Wiggins Pass inlet

Food and Drink within a short drive of Barefoot Beach

- Doc's Beach House; 3.5 out of 5 on Trip Advisor; gulf view; dine inside or outside; adjacent to the "hole in the hedge" or access from the beach; $$$

- Coconut Jack's Waterfront Grille; 4.0 out of 5 on Trip Advisor; bay front; boat access; dine inside or outside; just east of the big turn on the north side of Bonita Beach Road; $$$$

- Fish House; 4.0 out of 5.0 on Trip Advisor; canal front; boat access; dine inside or outside; on the right side about a half mile after you leave the Dragon Tower.   There is satellite parking just east of the restaurant;$$$

Vanderbilt Beach Park and Delnor Wiggins State Park

Directions

- Go directly west from I75 along Immokalee Rd to reach Delnor Wiggins Park. The exit # is 111. No turning required.
- To reach Vanderbilt Beach Park turn left on Route 41 and right on Vanderbilt Beach Rd.
- Take 41 North from Naples and turn left at Vanderbilt Beach Rd. (just after the Pelican Bay neighborhood). The parking garage will be on your left.

Parking	🌴🌴🌴🌴🌴
Food, Drink, Amenities	🌴
Toilets/Change Rooms/Showers	🌴🌴🌴
Rentals	🌴🌴🌴🌴
Shelling	🌴
Proximity and variety of off-site amenities	🌴🌴🌴🌴🌴

Vanderbilt Beach is the Big Kahuna of Naples beaches. It is the easiest beach to find for a variety of reasons, not the least of which is that the road that takes you directly there is named for it and if you should have to ask for directions everyone in town has been there at least once. At a little under three miles it is among the longer stretches of strand that I have delineated and you can get to Clam Pass from here by walking two miles to the left. As well, it is really two beaches combined - Vanderbilt Beach and Wiggins Beach. There are big hotels operated by chains, smaller family owned motels and hotels as well as posh restaurants, elegant condominiums, single family mansions and old fashioned family beach houses. The latter are often of the pre-pretentious era of the 1950's and 1960's when you didn't have to be a multi-millionaire to have a place on the beach and 1,500 square feet of air conditioned space was considered big enough. At the northern end of this stretch about halfway to the end from the Vanderbilt Beach entrance begins Delnor Wiggins State Park at 111th Ave. which is an extension of Immokalee Road to the west of Route 41. To further obfuscate things someone decided to call the last section before the park entrance a third name, Bluebill Ave. This entrance is about 5 miles west of Exit 111 on I75, if you are coming in for the day. It's a straight line all the way in, so just ignore the street names and keep on driving until you come to the parking kiosk.

There is no direct exit from I75 onto Vanderbilt Beach Road so you'll have to come from either the north or the south at either Exit 111 or Exit 107. You can enter the beach itself from public land at the north and south ends, and the two public parks which are under two different government jurisdictions act like book ends for the "beachiest" of Naples beaches. By this is I am implying a mix of public and private enterprise where conservation meets business and in essence forms a brackish business estuary that is neither the Jersey Shore nor Keewaydin Island. You can actually engage in a noisy water sport and the patrons are here to have a good time. This is likely the most boisterous group of beachgoers in the county and if it is hard, lithe, glistening bodies you seek as an alternative to the study of the nesting habits of terns, then this is the beach for you. As drinking alcoholic beverages is legally proscribed here, (given the amount of visible consumption you'd think it was prescribed) much of the boisterousness comes from the ready availability of the former at business establishments very nearby. If you choose to join the imbibers here, keep in mind that the consumption of alcoholic beverages on this beach is subject to a hefty fine from the periodically patrolling county park ranger. The push and pull of these two elements, conservation and business, are regularly seen in news stories of political battles to improve the public facilities and ambitious plans for piers, bathrooms and viewing decks are regularly defeated. Finally in 2014 a substantial renovation and improvement to the restrooms was completed, though more ambitious plans for observation decks and a fishing pier have been shelved. Additionally, Vanderbilt Beach is unique among local beaches in that this is where the public use and private beach access issues are the most contentious and the battle is fought along this stretch more often than anywhere else outside of New Jersey. Private land owners who have invested millions of dollars in their enterprises try to maintain an aura of exclusivity for their privileged clientele. The proletariat usually insists that it has a constitutionally protected right to the "beach" often simply expressed as "there are no private beaches in Florida". The plutocracy would "beg to differ" but of course plutocrats rarely beg and just hire lawyers instead. The public's right to the beach begins with the Roman Emperor Justinian who wrote in the Corpus Juris Civilis in 529 AD that "By the law of nature these things are common to all mankind, the air, running water, the sea and consequently the shores of the sea." One thousand, four hundred and eighty six years later all we can say is "what's the problem"? In truth, all of Justinian's elements have been the subject for war combatants and litigants throughout the world for most of those thousand plus years and likely they aren't done yet. If you are already annoyed about having your beach rights infringed upon, remind me to plan to be somewhere else when they go after our Justinian right to the air we breathe. Generally speaking the law has evolved to mean that people can walk laterally across a beach to seaward of the mean high water mark and plunk their butts in the sand similarly. It is ironic is it not, that a man from Byzantium is indirectly and inadvertently responsible for the byzantine nature of this country's beach access laws.

The part of Vanderbilt Beach that is run by the County Parks and Recreation Department is another one of those good news and bad news deals. While there is a lot of parking available (340 spaces in the garage alone) as well as scores more on street side spaces and private lots, this beach is so popular they all fill up fast on busy days. I am always reminded of a famous Yogi Berra quote "Nobody goes there anymore; it's too crowded". So that's the bad news. If you can't get into the garage here take a right turn and drive north on Gulfshore Drive past the Vanderbilt Beach Resort to Bluebill Ave. where you can try the state park. There are 5 parking lots here for a total of over 200 spaces. Since Collier County or Naples City Beach stickers are not valid here there is often space available before noon as many frugal locals are not interested in paying for something that is free at every other beach access. The entrance fee is $6.00 and uniquely they do allow dogs on a short leash in the park but not on the beach. There are also grills to barbecue, good facilities with showers and change rooms and a boat launch. Located here is the only hard bottomed coral reef north of the Keys on this section of coast where you can snorkel or scuba. The reef is not marked, but is roughly between 200 and 300 feet due west from parking lot #2. The water depth is 10 to 15 feet, so don't forget a float and a dive flag as you can be vulnerable to passing boats that are running too close to shore. Search YouTube for some videos about this site. This is also one of the few beaches where there is ample shade from big mature Australian pine trees that can offer a welcome respite from the blazing Florida sun. When my grandson Jack was a baby and my favorite dog Molson was a nonagenarian this wonderful park offered something for both. There is also a parking lot about a half mile to the east on Bluebill, just over the bridge. The intention here is for you to drop your stuff and passengers at the turn-around next to the Moraya Bay Beach Tower and then have you drive out of the area and walk back in. The turn-around and a new public restroom recently replaced a small county owned parking lot at the public access just outside the gate of the state park. The traffic here on a holiday can be so bad, a county Sheriff's Deputy is required to direct traffic and like Yogi, I just wouldn't go there on a holiday unless it was really early in the morning. The Moraya Bay Beach Tower whose most famous seasonal resident is Sean Hannity of Fox cable TV fame was a controversial development of its own a few years back. It replaced a very popular seaside motel with a Chickee Hut bar and nightly poolside entertainment of the Jimmy Buffett kind. By the way, in my lexicon a Chickee Hut and a Tiki Hut are the same but different in that the former is native Floridian and made exclusively by Seminoles and the latter is Polynesian. Not all Tiki's are Chickee's, but all Chickee's are Tiki's. Let's see Yogi get his tongue around that one. If you want to see a lot of them in one place, check out the Chickee photo in the Marco Island section.

You could hardly blame the owner of the Vanderbilt Inn for selling out his five acres at the peak of the real estate boom in 2006 for $71.6 million dollars but of course some people did. The local online news comment columns were full of people that decried the loss of ever more native cracker habitat. You would have to sell a lot of tequila in Margaritaville to make that kind of dough, but Come Monday you'd be either eating the Last Mango in Paris or that Cheeseburger in Paradise as you mulled over whether you'd made enough money to buy Miami. Certainly you couldn't be blamed for thinking of yourself as one lucky pirate turning forty. There are 72 condominium units in Moraya Bay Beach Tower that have sold for between $2.0 and $4.0 million each. As you might expect, it wasn't long until these new land rush settlers tried to establish their claim to the sand, by delineating their private space on the beach. That caused a kerfuffle that led to the need for the local citizenry to consult their dog eared copies of Corpus Juris Civilis after which they were able to resume their bronzing unmolested.

There is good fishing in Wiggins Pass and just a few yards north across the pass is the southern end of Barefoot Beach. If swimming were permitted and safe you could get there in a few minutes. As it is, you can get there by car from here though it's complicated and a lot easier with a boat which by the way you are able to launch at Delnor Wiggins Park for an additional $5.00 fee or east on the river at the county ramp for an $8.00 fee. Annual county boat launch ramp fees are $75.00 but you can't use them in state parks.

Meanwhile back at the south end at Vanderbilt Beach, the same dynamics are in play and issues similar to those at the Moraya Bay Tower also play themselves out in the sand in front of the Ritz Carlton. The farther you walk

south, the closer you are to escaping the madness though in this case it takes

some doing as there is a half mile long gauntlet of first plebeians and then

plutocrats that must be run. The interesting thing is that in this context where the

usual trappings of wealth are not evident in their nearly natural state, you can't

tell the person that owns the pipeline from the person who welded it and on this

stretch of beach it is likely you will encounter both. If you have made it this far

you are now on Pelican Bay Beach and ready for the next chapter.

Food and Drink within walking distance of Vanderbilt Beach Park

---

	• Buzz's Lighthouse; 3.5 out of 5.0 on Trip Advisor; canal view; dine inside or outside; ½ block north of the Vanderbilt Beach drop-off and across the street; $$
	• Turtle Club; 4.5 out of 5.0 on Trip Advisor; gulf view; dine inside or outside; Located in the Vanderbilt Beach Resort on the west side of the road across from Lighthouse or access from the beach; $$$$
	• The Beach Box Café; 4.0 out of 5.0; no view; dine outside or take out; new in 2015; directly across the street from the beach; $
	• Gumbo Limbo; 4.5 out of 5.0 on Trip Advisor; gulf view; dine inside or outside; located in the Ritz Carlton Resort about ½ mile south of the Vanderbilt Beach drop-off; $$$
	• La Playa – Tiki Bar and Grill; 4.5 out of 5.0 on Trip Advisor; gulf view; dine inside or outside; located in La Playa Resort about ½ mile north of the Turtle Club; $$$$

This place is so crowded nobody goes there anymore

The Ritz Carlton is on the upper left and Bay Colony buildings in Pelican Bay toward the center.

In 2014 sand was trucked in from inland quarries, rather than pumped ashore from the Gulf of Mexico by marine dredgers. The move was controversial for a number of reasons, the most notable of which was the impact from thousands of dump truck trips on residential streets and the fact the texture and color of the quarried sand was different than the dredged sand. Government officials claimed to have matched the sand as best they could and after months of wave action, it is increasingly difficult to tell the difference, though it was clearly different in the first days of its application.

Just one of many idyllic beachside picnic groves at Delnor Wiggins

Delnor Wiggins Park beach with a view towards Vanderbilt Beach in the south. Notice the many Australian pines (Casuarinas) on the left which provide much of the shade for the picnic groves

Delnor Wiggins Park with a view toward the north east. The no swimming boat channel is on the left and the trees in the upper left are at the south end of Barefoot Beach

Imagining a perfect day at the beach

One of many special needs equipped facilities buildings at Delnor Wiggins

Residential developments that are distant from a beach sometimes opt to run shuttles. This is the 4:45 PM return run for the Spanish Wells neighborhood in neighboring Bonita Springs. The Windstar development in southeast Naples on the "beach less" bay also runs a shuttle service to Keewaydin Island.

Pelican Bay Beach (north of Clam Pass to Vanderbilt)

Parking	
Food, Drink, Amenities	
Toilets/Change Rooms/Showers	
Rentals	
Shelling	🌴🌴🌴🌴🌴
Proximity and variety of off-site amenities	

There are no driving directions to this beach, as there is strictly limited automobile access from the landward side. In the few instances where there is, the area is gated with 24/7 security. The above table is accurate only if you are a member of the general public and just exercising your Justinian right to walk along the beach here and not a guest of a Pelican Bay member. All property owners are required to be members of the Pelican Bay Foundation and if you are lucky enough to be one, or know one, are visiting with one or renting a unit for the year, a month or the season, then go ahead and fill up this table with 5

🌴 's in each box. So if you don't have a friend who owns property in Pelican Bay just yet, run out and find one for yourself as soon as possible or just go ahead and buy a place in there. Compared to everything else around, it's not that expensive. If you do, you'll be able to boast that this stretch of sand is your "private beach" even though between you and I and Justinian we know it is not.

For the rest of us, this is a walking beach if ever there was one as there is no parking and no public facility of any sort. There are dense crowds of people at both the north and south ends of this 2 ½ mile stretch of sand, depending on where you start and the time of year, but if you walk ten or fifteen minutes from either end you will be transported to a totally different world. Remember, that if you are entering this beach from the south, you will need to wade through or swim across Clam Pass the water depth and current of which fluctuates hourly with the wind, tide and the weather. The Pelican Bay Foundation, the master Home Owners' Association (HOA) responsible for this area is a federation of 93 separate and distinct condominiums and HOA's within the 2,100 acre neighborhood, comprised of residences from about $300,000 up to $20,000,000 or more. The master HOA operates a south (Sandbar) and a north (Marker 36) beach club facility for its members and access from the eastern land side is strictly monitored to limit use to residents and their guests. Recently, I took part-time work as one of those monitors, where we scan membership cards into a database to determine people's eligibility to use the common areas. Everyone coming to the beach from the east, either on a tram or by foot is required to present foundation issued ID. Renters, tenants and guests may be issued either free or paid identification, but identification is required. The master HOA operates a large fleet of over forty battery powered golf cart limousines that transport their members and guests over the mangrove estuary and out to the beach. About 13,000 people call the Pelican Bay development home at least some of the time and each residence pays annual dues to the master association of about $1,600 which among many benefits results in their never having to schlep stuff to the beach in addition to never having to drive there or pay for a parking spot. In and of itself this seems like a nice perk for about $4.00 a day never mind the free canoes, kayaks, sailboats, cabanas, lounge chairs, umbrellas and the right to enjoy a legal cocktail on the beach. Who said "Membership has its privileges"?

From Clam Pass north on the beach, past the Sandbar Club to the first house, is a pristine 1.2 miles of an anomalous Robinson Crusoe experience in the middle of a densely populated urban environment. Walking north from Clam Pass you will pass the Sandbar Club (members and guests only) and then you'll walk past the new Marker 36 Restaurant (formerly the Sandpiper and also members and guests only) which has six large screen TV's and a backlit bar that seats about 50 people and is so-named because its located adjacent to that Beach Marker. The Sandbar Club is at Marker 41 so the distance between the two is exactly 5,000 feet or just under a mile which as you will recall from grade school is 5,280 feet.

This is as good a place as any to discuss the beach marker system in use in Collier County. It is a state wide system administered by the Department of

Environmental Protection (DEP) that places a lettered and numbered sign at 1,000 foot intervals along the sandy shores of the state. In Collier County it begins with R001 at the Lee County line and ends with R148 at Cape Marco which is on the north side of Caxambas Pass. While its primary purpose is as part of a coastline management system, it is used very effectively by the beach patrols and emergency responders for everything from locating sea turtle nests, to rescuing injured wildlife and stricken visitors and now apparently for naming restaurants. If you are following closely and are somewhat geeky you might decide to do the math and immediately realize that Pelican Bay's north beach club, restaurant and bar is 36,000 feet from Doc's Beach House and the hole in the hedge. If you take the 148,000 linear feet of beach and divide by 5,280 to get the mileage equivalent, you will notice that it comes to 28 miles. Since, the subtitle of this book claims to cover 35 miles of beaches, where are the other seven miles? Well when you add the beaches on the outer Ten Thousand Islands without bridges the longest of which is the Dickman's, Kice, Morgan, Carr, Cape Romano archipelago at 5 miles we get to 33. All the rest of the islands without bridges and the inside keys with shell and sand landings such as Helen's, Coon, Panther, Brush, Whitehorse, easily total two more miles together and thus my math says that there are 35 miles of beaches in this county. My college major however was not math, but political science so if someone who majored in engineering or geography or something similar would like to take issue with the calculations, feel free to do so. Most of the promotional literature excludes the less accessible island beaches so that's my story and I am sticking to it. It was frankly surprising that there was no reference to this particular number in my research. It might be that the local promoters wanted you to believe that there was an infinite amount of beach and exaggerating beach length (like fish length) is not without precedent as the famous Seven Mile Beach in Grand Cayman is really only 5.5 miles long. Collier County Parks and Recreation seems to prefer a 17 mile number which as it turns out is the mileage from the north county line to Gordon Pass, which as you will discover in this book does not include any island beaches.

The first house you come to after Marker 36 will be one of only a dozen beachfront single family homes in Pelican Bay in an exclusive enclave called the Strand that itself sits inside the secured Bay Colony neighborhood at Pelican Bay. Ten or twenty million dollars (what the heck who's counting) wouldn't be out of line for one of these spectacular isolated homes with water on two sides and two miles of beach in each direction. Public records indicate that one sold in 2008 for $12 million which was likely at the nadir of local real estate prices after the national bubble burst. In 2014 one of these rarely offered homes was on the market for $19.9 million and if you plan on buying it with your lottery winnings, do bear in mind that you need to set aside an additional $15,000 or more monthly for property taxes and association fees. Shelling here is excellent as few people walk this way and some days the dune and scarp line is so steep and high that you can't see a single building even when you look for them. Considering that there are two dozen or so condominium towers some as high as 20 stories just a half mile to the east, we ought to recognize this as an astounding feat of environmental and social engineering. There is a kayak cross-over at beach marker R37 which corresponds roughly to marker 25 on the Clam Pass Canoe Trail on the estuary side, if you are coming or going by small paddle craft. The landing on the estuary side is very muddy here though and I don't recommend it at low tide, unless you are game for a stinky mud bath to your knees or thighs. However, paddling to this spot on the canoe trail from the Clam Pass parking lot free non-motorized boat launch, saves you a long walk and a possible swim and puts you directly into your Robinson Crusoe experience without having to step over a lot of bodies, even in season. Here, you should sit and mull over your options. North is a lot more walking (unless you have called ahead to have a friend pick you up at the Vanderbilt garage). South you can get back through Clam Pass in good time and take a tram ride back to the public lot at the foot of Seagate Dr. West is out as it is a very long swim to Texas. East is the low tide mud bath. Assuming you chose north, after you pass the Strand beach houses and ask yourself why you never worked for a company that granted stock options, the first tall buildings you come to on the beach are part of the Bay Colony group which as the name suggests is an elite enclave within the Pelican Bay community that has nothing to do with Pilgrims and everything to do with financial success. Among many, one of the more famous residents here is Judge Judy who I am told lives in one of the penthouses. We end this segment at the Gumbo Limbo restaurant on the beach at the Ritz Carlton, Naples. The

gumbo limbo is a native tree that has thin red, skin-like bark that often appears

to be peeling. For that reason, it is often slyly referred to as the "tourist tree".

Remember that you do still have to walk back, or not. By road along the

Tamiami Trail it is about a 2.5 mile cab ride back to your car in the Clam Pass

parking lot.

The view from the north side of Clam Pass at Pelican Bay beach looking south toward Clam Pass Park with Seagate and Park Shore Beaches in the distance

Marker 36 Restaurant and Bar. You may use this private club only as a guest of a friend or family member who lives in the neighborhood or if you are renting on a long or short term basis from an owner. So while it is private, it is not really all that exclusive as a rough estimate suggests that a hundred thousand people or more likely qualify to use it each season. As Groucho Marx once said, "Please accept my resignation. I don't want to belong to any club that will have me as a member".

Looking north to the Sandbar Club at Pelican Bay.

The same beach on a different day.

Black Skimmers head to wind among other terns, gulls and pelicans at a Clam Pass sandbar. It is considered very bad form to rouse these birds into flight as when they are resting like this they are restoring much needed energy for migratory flight. Please try to resist the urge to scatter them and ask your children to do the same.

Clam Pass Beach (Clam Pass south to Seagate Beach)

Directions

- Exit 107 West off I75 or take Tamiami Trail north or south to Pine Ridge Rd.
- When you cross west of Route 41 at the Barnes and Noble book store, Pine Ridge Rd. becomes Seagate Dr.
- When Seagate Dr. bends south (left) in less than a mile, continue on straight to the parking lot. You will need $8.00 for the daily parking fee or a valid beach parking permit, available free to residents and property owners of Collier County
- If you turn left at Seagate Dr. you will end up at Seagate Beach with no facilities instead of at Clam Pass Park.
- The address of the hotel adjacent to the park's parking lot, Naples Grande Beach Resort is 475 Seagate Dr. You can plug this into your favorite navigation "app" to reach your perfect beach.

Parking	🌴🌴🌴🌴🌴
Food, Drink, Amenities	🌴🌴🌴🌴🌴
Toilets/Change Rooms/Showers	🌴🌴🌴🌴🌴
Rentals	🌴🌴🌴🌴
Shelling	🌴🌴🌴
Proximity and variety of off-site amenities	🌴

A lot of confusion surrounds this area. In addition to being a beach, it is

also a park, a conservation area, a luxury beach resort, a nature tour on a

boardwalk and a parking lot located more than half a mile east of the gulf while

the beach that everyone is looking for is nowhere visible upon arrival. It's no

wonder people are confused before they even get here. To make matters

more interesting a private home owners' association (HOA) known as the

Pelican Bay Foundation (see the previous chapter) exercises some control over

the use of much of the land that is not part of the park and from time to time

finds itself as gatekeeper so to speak to other people's interests. A case in point

is water access to the gulf for the 80 or 90 homeowners in the Seagate

neighborhood, the majority of the homes of which are on canals with only

limited access to the gulf as a result of shallow channels, navigation markers that

are not Coast Guard approved, an inlet that's barely passable and rarely

dredged and a funky drawbridge that requires the bridge operator to commute

from wherever in town he might be at the time of the call. The luxury beach

resort called the Naples Grande that is owned and operated by a Real Estate

Investment Advisory group called Northwood provides free transportation from

the parking lot to the beach to all comers….overnight guests of the resort or not.

Northwood also owns the New York Palace, the Boston Revere and the Cheeca

Lodge in the Florida Keys among other properties. They recently changed the

name from the Waldorf Astoria Naples after they purchased the property from

the Blackstone Group, majority owners of the Hilton hotel brands. There is also a private boat storage area for Pelican Bay residents (kayaks, canoes and paddleboards) adjacent to a public launch area for non-motorized boats. The public is encouraged to use the launch area (no trailers or motors), but not allowed to store their vessels in the racks. The hotel's operators (which at one time included the Miami billionaire Wayne Huizenga who founded three Fortune 500 companies) have historically run the concession at the beach under various names such as The Registry Resort, the Waldorf Astoria Naples and the Naples Grande Beach Resort continuously for more than a quarter of a century. While their stated philosophy is to treat all visitors to the beach as its guests, irrespective of whether they happen to be renting a room at the time, they do have a contractual obligation to the county government which involves annual payments and services that include transportation to the beach for county guests....thus the free tram ride.

I have spoken with people who have lived in Naples for twenty years and had never visited this place. The confusion with regard to this well kept secret appears to be the result of its special location at the south end of the Pelican Bay neighborhood, the beaches of which are thought to be inaccessible to the public. The neighborhood per se includes everything west of the Tamiami Trail (Route 41), north of Seagate Dr. and south of Vanderbilt Beach Road and the hotel itself is a member of the Pelican Bay HOA. Within the larger 2,100 acre neighborhood there are 570 acres of green space designed to protect the mangroves trees and containing an interesting and easy canoe and kayak trail that has one way in and one way out. There are regular letters to the editor of the local newspaper decrying this state of affairs (lack of public access to the beach here), yet Clam Pass Park was created and donated to the public by the developers of Pelican Bay (then known as Westinghouse Communities and later WCI) precisely to give access to the public to those same Pelican Bay beaches. The beaches immediately north and south of Clam Pass are equally terrific in all respects. Despite that though, the topography suggests to some non-resident visitors that they are missing out as they would have to wade or swim across a channel to the north where blue beach umbrellas abound at the residents' so-called South Beach club. Access to these beaches is indeed restricted from the eastern land side. Pelican Bay's residents use the area north of the Pass and the public uses the area south of the Pass. For the purposes of this chapter, I am defining Clam Pass Beach as that area south of Clam Pass inlet and north of Seagate Dr. The area immediately north of Clam Pass is accessible to the public after a two mile walk from the north at Vanderbilt Beach and from the south via a ten or twenty yard wade or swim depending on the tide and the current. This effectively does create a barrier to entry for a large part of the population, but it is what it is and generally speaking it is very, very good. Some pretty smart people figured this out back in the day.

The actual park as administered by the Collier County Parks and Recreation department runs 3,000 linear feet from the inlet south to the Naples Cay condominiums. There has been discussion and conjecture about extending the Clam Pass boardwalk south to a point near the Seagate Beach Access on Park Shore Beach, thus opening much more of the southern terrain of the park's beach to use. Since this would inevitably involve the destruction of mangrove trees which have been protected by the state of Florida since 1982, there are some significant hurdles for this plan to overcome. As the Pelican Bay Foundation is also charged with mangrove preservation as part of its purview it appears unlikely that it would approve of the expansion, but one never knows. Meanwhile, back at the Clam Pass parking lot there are currently designated spaces for 180 or so cars but they have been known to cram up to 200 cars on busy holidays. There has also been discussion about putting another parking garage here which would double or triple the parking spaces, but unless they change or dramatically improve the process of moving the people from the parking lot to the beach, this doesn't make a lot of sense, as there are already long lines waiting at the tram station even without a garage.

Once you've parked the car you should walk to the northwest corner of the lot where there is a gazebo structure that serves as a depot for the seven passenger golf cart stretch limousines that are used by the Naples Grande hotel to shuttle Clam Pass Park visitors and hotel guests to the beach. Just recently renovated the gazebo had contained a sizeable colony of Brazilian free-tailed bats for a decade or more. An alternative bat house was installed in the adjacent freshwater marshland by the parks department just to the east of their old house. While as of this writing they haven't taken up residence in their new digs yet it is hoped that they will, as they did an admirable job of keeping the mosquito population in this large saltwater marsh under control. It was time for the bats to move as their colony was regularly harassed by people and crows alike.

Likely because they are powered by electric motors, the vehicles are referred to as trams, but they are battery powered and there are no overhead or underground wires to drive the motors as with the trams of old. The distance to the beach is a little more than half a mile, 0.625 of a mile to be exact. You are free to measure it yourself on Google Earth using the path tool. Amusingly, the county officially says the boardwalk is three quarters of a mile long, 0.750 and the hotel regularly tells its guests it is a half a mile, 0.50. Of course the hotel has a vested interest in reassuring its patrons that it is closer to the beach and the county has a vested interest in having its patrons feel that they are getting more board-walk for their tax dollars. No doubt, as with all communications from corporate and government entities, the truth lies somewhere in between.

There are three beach access boardwalks in the Pelican Bay neighborhood but the other two as discussed are for residents only. This one was designated from the outset for the use of hotel guests and the general public. The other two boardwalks have wooden surfaces, though the wood is premium Ipe, (pronounced epay) in the case of the Pelican Bay ones. This one has composite plastic lumber made from 4.32 million recycled milk jugs among other things. It is easy on the feet much of the time but it is blazingly hot in

summer and will burn your feet if you aren't wearing shoes and it can be very

slippery when wet.   On a hot summer day in 2012, I measured the temperature

of a plastic board in the sunlight with an infrared temperature gun. It registered

148 degrees. During the summer months, local teens like to dare each other to

see how far they can get in their bare feet. There are also sixty-eight thousand

stainless steel screws embedded in it and that many screw heads to be wary of

when walking, though the county undertook to reinstall all of them in 2011 and

properly countersink the heads below the surface. Of course I was present

during the construction and the foreman gave me the number. How else would

I know? Surely you didn't think I had counted them all though we once had a

tram driver from Michigan who counted all the boards.

The walk from the gazebo to the beach is a pleasant twelve to fifteen

minutes while the tram ride is about three or four minutes depending on the

tram's driver, the pedestrian traffic and the condition of the batteries of the

particular vehicle you are on. Many of the drivers will provide a short nature tour

of the mangrove estuary and have received a modicum of training from the

Conservancy of Southwest Florida volunteer guides. If you are pleased with the

tour, the conversation or the heat beating complimentary ride to the beach,

the drivers get paid less than summer camp counselors and while prohibited

from soliciting gratuities they may accept them if voluntarily offered. For those

who want a bigger dose of the flora and fauna, the Conservancy's volunteer guides provide a 60-90 minute led nature tour six days a week (Sundays excepted) from December to April. If you like spiders then this tour is for you as the pathway is often framed with intricate banana spider and spiny orb weaver webs, especially in the autumn. Something about Halloween seems to bring them out, though I am sure this is only coincidence, or is it?

The maximum peak passenger capacity provided for this shuttle service is 210 people per hour, and that capacity has to be shared with the hotel tram stop. Before 11:00 AM and after 4:00 PM they usually run at fewer than 100 passengers per hour. If there are more than 50 people on line it might be quicker to walk out, as you don't want to blow off quality beach time wasting away at the caddie shack when Margaritaville beckons just a kilometer away. Besides you will earn bragging rights among your friends as not many people can claim to have walked a kilometer on a bed of 4.3 million burning hot milk jugs. Once while on a road trip from Munich to Zurich I stayed overnight in Liechtenstein just for the bragging rights. In the evening at the forlorn bar, I introduced a couple of Teutonic types to the rituals of tequila shots by explaining that the mysterious dusty, sealed bottle of hitherto neglected clear liquor on the top shelf contained "Mexican Schnapps". Not even the bartender knew what it was. According to her, it had just always been there. Many years later I have yet to meet anyone who has even stayed the night in Liechtenstein, let alone someone who introduced a new pastime to an entire country and generation. Frankly I don't think I have received appropriate recognition for my contributions to the globalization of 20th century Liechtenstein.

So you have arrived at the beach on the tram. There are a couple of steps up to the deck (there is a ramp if you prefer) and if someone in your party has a physical disability there is a beach wheelchair available for use free of charge. This has big round tires engineered for beach sand so someone has to be able to push it as it cannot be self-propelled. If a friend or family member is wheel chair bound, you can request a special tram that has a folding ramp to allow the chair and the occupant to ride without having to maneuver the person out of the chair. The restrooms are also up to code with respect to handicap accessibility. If it is winter and you are a normal human being from somewhere else presumably north of here, this is where you ought to experience your first real WOW factor at a Collier County beach. The view from the deck here is nothing short of breath taking and looks like a photograph that might have been the cover shot for Coastal Living magazine. The sky will be azure, the sand blindingly white, the sea turquoise, the waves capped with white foam. When the sea breeze is blowing from the southwest, I call it a "CeeBreeze." That's because a day or two ago this same wind was blowing over Cuba, Cozumel, Cancun, Campeche, or the Caymans depending on the southern angle. Get it? They all start with the letter "C" which rhymes with "SEA".

At this moment you are standing about 1,000 miles due east of Brownsville TX and South Padre Island. What ought to strike you next is that while this is a public park, there is no indication of that here. By which I mean there is no rustic log furniture, stone walls or generic brown paint and there are no government employees. This deck is effectively (though not legally), a lease hold of the Naples Grande Beach Resort and in the tradition of "Mi casa es su casa", their furniture is your furniture. This of course, only applies to the furniture on the deck, not on the beach. All of the staff here including the chefs, servers, beach attendants, tram drivers and housekeepers (the bathrooms are cleaned every two hours all day long), are hotel staff. If for some reason they are not treating you as if you were a hotel guest, feel free to call the hotel or the Parks department and complain. There are a dozen stools lined up for you to sit and watch the waves, much like the stools at Nepenthe's in Big Sur that overlook the Pacific. I would rate that spot as one of the most spectacular views in the country while I would rate this one as among the most serene. So, if you were to stay right here within a few feet of the bar, the restrooms and the tram ride back nobody would hold it against you. Just as there are people who live in Naples and have never been here, there are people who spend hours every day on this deck doing crosswords and drinking coffee or water or beer or whatever and rarely if ever set foot in the sand or the water.

Of course our more intrepid readers will want to head out onto the sand. You have a choice of left or right. The route to the right will take you for a short quarter mile walk to Clam Pass. As with most beach explorations it is best to visit this at low tide as the sand bars, mud flats and sand spits are more exposed. Additionally, as this inlet is approved for swimming, when the tide does turn to flood, then your ride on the current will be inbound and you won't end up in Brownsville. Actually, the pass is so narrow and the sandbar so extensive, there is little likelihood that you will be swept out to sea here, but it can feel like it and periodically panic ensues and bad things happen. Please be prudent and wary of currents and riptides. Until it is dredged again however, the water is not likely to be over your head though. Most other passes in Collier you should avoid swimming in. Those on the mainland are marked for the most part but many of the island passes are not. The pass between Dickmans and Kice islands can generate white water at peak flow. If you are floating in Clam Pass, once the tidal current has pulled you into the mangroves, find a tidal mud flat or sand spit to make your exit and then walk back to the beach and do it all over again. People have been doing this here for generations. There was even a big old tree to swing from and drop into the current. The parks department has severely trimmed the tree back in its concern that someone was going to get hurt, but the rope keeps reappearing and on my most recent trip there in March of 2015, the rope swing was back up and functioning as good as ever.

Back in the day, before there was a park, a boardwalk or a tram there was a beach road from the end of Seagate Drive just behind the dune line that people used to drive their cars on to get to this spot. There is a vestige of that road which is about 80 yards long that runs parallel to the beach. It can be found northwest of the restaurant under the biggest sea-grape bush you will likely ever see. This is in and of itself always a delightful little walk upon which you are likely to encounter a big old gopher tortoise. The road now ends at the beach where there have been recent extensive plantings of sea oats. If you follow the path through the sea oats you will find a nice little sunny spot in the lee of the mangroves that can make a winter's day with a cold north wind, quite pleasant indeed. Long time locals have told me that there was a large grove of Australian pines (Casuarinas) here that blanketed the area with soft pine needles making it a great campsite. The problem is that the blanket of needles smothers anything indigenous that is trying to grow underneath it. As an invasive, exotic species they were all removed from here by the environmental stewards of the conservation area. If you are interested in knowing what they look like, there is still a windbreak stand of them on the south side of the parking lot and there continue to be large stands of them on the various island beaches. Once again, this is where the tide becomes a factor. If it is low and ebbing you might choose to wade through to the Land of Oz on the other side. That is the so-called private beach of Pelican Bay after all and there is a five mile stretch of sand in front of you. In fact, after you get past the Sandbar Club, the first roughly mile and half of it has no buildings on it at all. Just remember the six hour tide cycle and that if you wade across when the water is waist deep, it might well be neck deep when you come back. Thus, if you are a competent swimmer dressed only in shorts and a tee shirt that won't present a problem. If however, you have taken a short break from a business conference at the Naples Grande and have rolled up your pants to wade through while holding your SmartPhone in your hand then the return journey has been known to cause a problem. One day, three young insurance executives all lost their cell phones to salt water damage. Also, do not cross the pass at the narrowest point. This is where the tidal current is strongest, where the erosion of the sand banks is most pronounced and thus where the drop off is most severe as the water flow scours the bottom. Look for passes in the water on the gulf side sandbar that while providing a more circuitous route offer a gentler more undulating path to the other side. The topography here changes daily, weekly and monthly. After the summer storms of 2012 a sandbar had almost completely closed the pass. The inlet was designed to be approximately 30 feet wide and 4 feet deep and will likely be dredged to that specification again in the relatively near future. If you are planning to cross the pass on foot do exercise caution and restraint. Annual water temperatures range from about 65 degrees in January to 90 degrees in August and the current can run from 0 to 5 knots in either direction. You ought to keep that in mind if you are wading across and swimming back on President's Day week-end.

Meanwhile we're back on the deck, basking in the sunshine and reveling in "las brisas" while tracking the progress of a pair of dolphins headed south. If we choose to follow along with them we have three miles of uninterrupted sand in this direction before we are blocked by the channel at Doctor's Pass. The first thing we'll notice is that left of the deck is where the hotel that gave us the free ride and the costly glass of wine (these things do tend to balance themselves out) stakes out its claim to the beach. It is public land and you are more than entitled to plunk your butt in the sand right in the middle of them. In fact, for a fee you are even able to use exactly the same chair and umbrella and play movie star for the day though this is Clam Pass Beach and not Miami's South Beach. Ironically though, the beach rental concessionaire Boucher Brothers is the very same company that handles the concession at the famous South Beach in the city of Miami Beach. They also rent stand up paddleboards and kayaks and sell a few sundries such as sun block and sand toys and they provide a big boat shaped sandbox for the kids. On off season summer week-ends the hotel discounts its rates and this section of beach might well be full of Miami families anyway who find the roughly 90 minute drive over Alligator Alley preferable to fighting the traffic, noise, congestion and the expense of visiting one of Miami's beaches which as everyone knows are not even in Miami. During the spring break season, the beach from here to the Pass will have more than a 1,000 people on it. Since few of them ever walk down to the southern extremities and the whole park as you will recall is only 3,000 linear feet, you can do the math and discern the challenge. So don't be shy, head south through the forest of logoed umbrellas to stake out your claim or rent one for yourself. Once again from here to the end of the park, there are no buildings. There are a couple of rock outcroppings that offer some lame snorkeling but for the most part this is just really nice beach. About a quarter mile south of the deck between Beach Markers R43 and R44 there is an old wooden footbridge to cross the dune line and follow a short cross-over path, intended for (but these days rarely used) by kayakers to Outer Clam Bay. It is fairly non-descript for a cross-over, but in my book sandy paths are always worth following. Over a period of time, one person or many have usually beaten a path for a reason and you might as well find out why for yourself. It is also one of the few places in this area that you can find free natural shade on this stretch of beach.

This old Clam Pass Tram station was razed in 2014. Before it was re-shingled the roof was made of cedar shakes and a large colony of Brazilian bats lived inside the copper peak, sometimes dropping guano on unsuspecting passengers below.

The new one as it appeared just before opening in the fall of 2014. It now has a metal roof.

Clam Pass in the winter of 2012 was plugged with sand. Its dredging is a constant battle of words between and among groups of environmentalists, politicians and homeowners. The tall buildings in the background are from left to right- the GLENVIEW, the STRATFORD and the ST. NICOLE just three of the 25 or so condo towers in the Pelican Bay neighborhood.

The bridge to nowhere at Clam Pass beach can be found between Marker R43 and R44. It appears to have been used as part of a cross-over trail from a kayak landing in Outer Clam Bay about 20 yards to the east.

Not your everyday road to the beach. This is the old trail northbound from the Naples Grande beach deck.

The only drawbridge in Collier County may well be among the world's smallest. There is a telephone number on the side of the bridge visible from the water and apparently if you call that number someone will be there within the hour to open it. I like to call it "Rube Goldberg inspired".

View of Clam Pass Park at low tide while looking north. The old road is in the trees to the right.

View of Clam Pass Park to the south. Naples Grande hotel guests hang out at the public beach here. The double bed lounges in the right foreground are rented for more than $100 a day.

Food and Drink at or nearby Clam Pass Park

- Rhode's End; not yet rated on Trip Advisor; dine outside only; gulf view; waterfront; located at Clam Pass Park Beach; $$$$
- Pelican Larry's Raw Bar and Grill; 3.5 out of 5 on Trip Advisor; dine inside or outside; located south east corner of Pine Ridge and Route 41; no view; $$
- The Catch of the Pelican; 4.5 out of 5.0 on Trip Advisor; dine inside or outside; pond view; located at Naples Grande Beach Resort; $$$$
- Brio Tuscan Grill; 4 out of 5 on Trip Advisor; no view; dine inside or outside; great happy hour; located at Waterside Shops; $$$$

Seagate, Park Shore, Moorings beaches (south from Seagate Drive to Doctors Pass)

Directions

- Use Exits #105 (Golden Gate Parkway) or Exit #107 (Pine Ridge Rd.) off I75
- From the north on Tamiami Trail (Route 41) turn right onto Park Shore Drive and drive to the end. Turn left (south) for Horizon Way, Vedado Beach and Miramar parking lots in that order. Turn right (north) to Seagate Beach parking lot.
- From the south on Tamiami Trail (Route 41) turn left onto Harbour Drive and drive to the end. Turn left (south) for Miramar parking lot and right (north) Vedado, Horizon Way and Seagate parking lots in that order.

Parking	🌴 🌴
Food, Drink, Amenities	
Toilets/Change Rooms/Showers	
Rentals	
Shelling	🌴 🌴
Proximity and variety of off-site amenities	🌴 🌴 🌴 🌴

This is another one of those tricky beaches to get to because it is a 2 mile long barrier island beach, though you'd likely never guess it when getting there from the north. The developers built a causeway out to the beach and then used a tiny seemingly less than adequate culvert to allow tidewater to flow between Venetian Bay and Outer Clam Bay, so you never get the idea that you've just arrived on an island. Of course, this allowed them to put in a fairly dense and expensive condo development called Naples Cay in what was likely a lost parcel of no-man's land between Park Shore and Clam Pass Park. There is a small lot for about three dozen cars at the end of Seagate Dr. and pedestrian only access to the beach at the end of Seagate Dr. accessible from Pine Ridge Rd. However there is no vehicle through access onto this section of Gulfshore Blvd. North, where there is another lot for about 40 cars to use the same access point just feet away and through the hedge. Like in Maine, you can't get there from here or here from there for that matter. Where the main access roads come into Park Shore the island definitely looks like an island as you can go over one of two stone bridges to cross the lagoons and canals. Both main roads, Park Shore Dr. and Harbour Dr. run west from the Tamiami Trail, so now that you know that, this beach is easy to find. Technically, a small section of less than a mile at the south end of this beach adjacent to Doctor's Pass is actually in the Moorings neighborhood and not Park Shore. Yes, Virginia there is a "u" in this spelling of harbor, so someone either went to school in the British Commonwealth or was just putting on airs.

As developments go, Park Shore is pretty impressive. It was proposed by the Lutgert family in the mid 1960's and was the first PUD (Planned Unit Development) in Collier County and developed over the next four decades. It covers 760 acres much of it water and likely wouldn't be approved today because of the environmental impact on the mangroves. If you tire of the sun and sand it is about a ten minute walk up the boulevard and across the street from the Vedado Beach or Horizon Way parking lots to get to Venetian Village. Here you can get some respite from the wind and waves and shop or lunch on the bayside lagoon or maybe use a restroom.

There is one irksome thing about this beach and that is the density of the high rise condominium towers that crowd the sand here. There is obviously nothing really wrong with it, as lots of great beaches share this characteristic (think Waikiki).   In fact, it obviously appeals to a lot of people as thousands of them have shelled out hundreds of thousands and even millions of dollars for a tiny piece of it in the form of a beachfront condominium with high maintenance fees. As of this writing the most expensive listing available is $15 million, but there are lots of listings in the single digit millions as well and this is AFTER the real estate bubble burst. Basketball legend and local golf course owner Larry Bird has owned a house on the bay here and medical mystery thriller write Robin Cook owns a penthouse on the beach here, so what do I know anyway? But there are 25 condominium towers strung along a two mile stretch of sand and I have to admit, this is what I don't like about it. We get quite used to that in big city waterfronts like Honolulu, Miami and Chicago and have come to expect it. But one doesn't expect it in Naples and Collier County and so it comes as a bit of a shock to the system. This beach is also relatively narrow and this wall of high rises, casts a long shadow before noon. I've walked this section, only a couple of times but there is a palpable feeling of encroachment and given the plethora of alternatives and the complete lack of public facilities in the area, I generally choose to go elsewhere. There is reasonably good fishing for sheepshead which is an excellent tasting fish that has generous "keeper" regulation limits on the north side of the rock jetty that delineates Doctor's Pass while there is good shelling and snorkeling on both the north and south side rock piles. You can buy live bait shrimp at the Park Shore Marina at the north end of Venetian Village or rent kayaks there as well. If you want to fish this region use the Miramar parking lot. At the opposite or north end of the beach where the county parking lots are, there are a couple of rock jetties where I have snorkeled and people also tend to fish and where my grandson posed with me for an excellent photograph once. There are three more public parking lots on this beach with about 40 spaces each that are south of the main bridges (Harbour Dr. and Park Shore Dr.) though there are no public restroom facilities at any of them. The three lots from south to north are called Miramar, Vedado and Horizon Way and they are some of the least known beach accesses in Naples. Now that you know how to find it, give it a try for yourself and let me know what you think

Seagate Beach with a view south towards Doctors Pass

On this blustery day in May, the gulf resembled Lake Michigan to make my grandson feel more at home. At high tide, these rocks are almost completely submerged and provide a place to fish and snorkel.

The Seagate Beach access path can be reached from the Seagate Drive county parking lot, as well as from Gulfshore Blvd. This site is a mile north of Venetian Village. Both routes culminate at cul de sacs, so you'll know when you have arrived.

Fishing on the northern rock jetty of Doctors Pass as viewed from the south side of the inlet. The closest parking lot to the fisherman is Miramar, operated by the City of Naples.

Food and Drink in Venetian Village

- Bayside Seafood Grill and Bar; 4.0 out of 5.0 on Trip Advisor; bay view; waterfront; dine inside or outside; $$$$
- The Village Pub;4.0 out of 5.0 on Trip Advisor; dine inside or outside; bay view; waterfront; $$
- MiraMare Italian Ristorante; 4.0 out of 5.0 on Trip Advisor; dine inside or outside; bay view; waterfront;$$$
- M Waterfront Grille; 4.5 out of 5.0 on Trip Advisor; bay view; waterfront; dine inside or outside; $$$$

Map Image provided by IslandMapstore.com, Copyright 2011 © Turrell, Hall and Associates

Naples Pier north to Doctor's Pass

Directions

- Take Exit 105 West off I75
- For Lowdermilk Park, turn left (south) on Tamiami Trail (Route 41) and then turn right (west) on Banyan Blvd. Proceed to the end of the road to enter the public parking lot.
- To access any other area along this stretch including the Naples Beach Hotel travel south (left) on Gulfshore Blvd. There will be parking lots at each avenue all the way to 33rd Ave. S.
- Gulfshore is called Gulfshore Blvd. N. until you get to Central Ave. after which it is called Gulfshore Blvd S.
- The pier is at 12th Avenue S., just after Broad Ave. The public parking lot is across the boulevard.

Parking	🌴🌴🌴🌴🌴
Food, Drink, Amenities	🌴🌴🌴🌴
Toilets/Change Rooms/Showers	🌴🌴🌴🌴🌴
Rentals	🌴🌴
Shelling	🌴
Proximity and variety of off-site amenities	🌴🌴🌴🌴🌴

Because of its location right in the center of Naples this stretch of strand is likely the one that hosts the most regular visitors and thus the one they will remember as most representative of Naples' area beaches. It encompasses a three mile long, languorously sweeping curve from the pier to the jetty at Doctor's Pass. This section includes the area around the pier that was first built in 1888, the venerable sprawling Naples Beach Resort that opened in 1946 and its beach side Sunset Beach Bar and Grill, Lowdermilk Park, the Edgewater Resort and the more or less private Moorings neighborhood beach where they won't let you park but don't stop you from sitting. There are also scores of waterfront condo's north of the Naples Beach hotel with architectural styles reminiscent of mid-20th century Acapulco. South of the hotel, one of the city of Naples building height restrictions takes effect which results in only single family beach homes from here on all the way down to Gordon Pass. The entire area is easily accessed from just about every avenue. Most avenues which run east to west (streets run north and south) dead-end at the beach. All of them have metered parking spaces ranging from a half dozen to two dozen or more and many have freshwater showers, shady rests and bicycle racks. Each year the Collier County government pays the City of Naples about a half a million dollars or more so residents of the county with beach stickers can park in both metered and non-metered spaces at no additional charge. If you are a Naples city resident you can keep your Hobie catamaran or Alden Ocean rowing shell right on the beach with an annual sticker purchased from the city. If you are a resident of some of the Lee County towns to the north without direct beach access, you might consider buying an annual sticker Collier County for $50.00 to get unlimited access to all of these beaches.

Unfortunately, this section of beach is studded with a great many large diameter storm water run-off pipes that create barriers to unimpeded walking along the beach. During the summer rainy season this can result in lots of fresh water running into the ocean, discoloring the inshore waters and impacting the salinity there. Fortunately, during the high winter dry season the impact on the seawater is benign and the pipes and their accompanying jetties act as groynes that deposit large piles of shells in their lee. They also make a great location for photo opportunities of children or grandchildren or both, standing on the pilings. The local authorities are under state government environmental pressure to do something else with the rainwater but their engineers have yet to devise an acceptable, cost effective alternative. The city of Naples is located for the most part on a peninsula with saltwater on three sides. What to do with the storm water run-off presents a conundrum here as it has nowhere else to go, short of piping it somewhere else which might prove hugely disruptive to its well heeled taxpayers. If when reading this book, you can think of something, I am sure they would be pleased to hear from you.

There are many opportunities for family activities on the beach here. At the pier itself (which is still open 24 hours at the time of writing) you can fish without a fishing license as the pier authority has a blanket license that applies to everyone. There are always large schools of baitfish around the pilings to observe and marvel over and of course the porpoises love to put on a show for the audience high above in the cheap seats. If the fish don't hold your attention the regular fishermen that resemble Hemingway characters and the visitors to the pier offer a passing parade of people of many nationalities, various body types and sartorial splendor or the lack thereof. Over on the adjacent beach the local high school students in their youthful vigor are skim boarding, surfing or kite surfing or playing a spirited game of volleyball. If the snack bar offerings on the pier don't interest you, it is a very short walk to the Third Street shopping district where multiple restaurants, shops and bars abound to suit all tastes. About seven avenue blocks north of the pier, it is also a short walk off the beach to the Fifth Ave. downtown shopping district which has over 7 street blocks of every shop and restaurant imaginable. The business district has sponsored as many as 14 events annually ranging from classic car shows to craft and art fairs as well as numerous parades and concerts.

There is only one public place for actual beachfront dining within Naples city limits and that is found on the site of the Naples Beach hotel about thirteen avenue blocks north of Fifth Ave. S. at 8th Ave. N. There are two restaurants and bars serving lunch, dinner and cocktails with entertainment most nights. In the off season the hotel also sponsors a jazz festival series on its magnificent grounds. The hotel recently completed a major renovation to enhance its beach side amenities and revamped its menu. This might be one of only places in the world where on a freezing day in Green Bay or Pittsburgh you can watch NFL football while dressed in nothing but flip flops and a bathing suit with the spouse and kids contently playing in the sand just a few yards away! I think this is what they had in mind when they called it the "Paradise Coast".

Not too far to the north of the hotel you will find the fore-mentioned Lowdermilk Park operated by the City of Naples. A children's play area on the lawn, volleyball courts, excellent comfort facilities and eight shady Chickee Huts on the sand (four on each side of the main pavilion) complete the picture. If you are in need of a break from the heat you can walk across the street to the First Watch restaurant in the retail development at Charleston Square and have a huge hearty breakfast, brunch or lunch at a reasonable price in air conditioned comfort. If finding a parking spot in the park presents a challenge on a Sunday morning in season just reverse the order, leave the car where it is and walk off your big breakfast to the park across the street. In season, this parking lot generally fills up by mid-morning, but there is overflow parking available on the adjacent street front. Metered spaces require a valid beach sticker or .25 cents per 10 minutes in quarters. The fine for a beach parking violation in the City of Naples is $37 which rises to $47 in ten days and much more after that. There is a lot of money at issue from these fees each year, so both the county and the city actively enforce their parking regulations.

.

View to the south along Naples Beach toward the Pier from Doctors Pass. This is a three mile curve. The pier is barely visible in the upper right hand corner of the picture. Notice the rock piles at intervals along the beach to contain the storm water drainage pipes.

Food and Drink at or nearby Naples City Beach

- First Watch; 4.5 out of 5.0 on Trip Advisor; dine inside or outside; waterfront; bay view; breakfast and lunch only; in Charleston Square across the Blvd from Lowdermilk Park; $$
- Sunset Beach Bar and Grill; 4.0 out of 5.0 on Trip Advisor; dine inside or outside; waterfront; gulf view; in the Naples Beach Resort; Entertainment Wed thru Saturday early evenings $$$
- HB's on the Gulf; 4.0 out of 5.0 on Trip Advisor; dine inside or outside; waterfront; gulf view; in the Naples Beach Resort; $$$$
- Tommy Bahama; 4.5 out of 5.0 on Trip Advisor; dine inside or outside; street view; 3 blocks directly behind the Pier on 3rd St.: $$$$$

Naples Pier to 32nd Ave. S.

Parking	🌴🌴
Food, Drink, Amenities	🌴🌴
Toilets/Change Rooms/Showers	🌴🌴🌴🌴🌴
Rentals	🌴
Shelling	🌴
Proximity and variety of off-site amenities	🌴🌴🌴

When you travel south of the pier there are about 20 blocks of very inviting and underutilized beach. Except for the private Port Royal Beach Club there are no commercial establishments or facilities here. Since parking is limited to the small lots at the avenue ends (the largest is located at 18th Ave. S.) and many of the fine residences stand empty most of the time, people using the beach are few and far between. For most of the rest of the stretch from 18th Ave. S., private beachfront estates limit public access and parking. For example, south of 20th where Gulfshore Blvd. ends and a crook in the road brings you to exclusive Gordon Dr., there is only one access path and that requires a somewhat lengthy walk from parallel parking spaces on Gordon. The homes and estates are magnificent and worth a gawk or two. For example, this stretch contains Naples most expensive home at $60 million. The landscaping on these estates can be exquisite and from time to time there are tall, old trees that spill their shade onto the beach and make this an appealing place to spend a few hours. For many years I observed a magnificent, Bermuda pink Georgian colonial that refused to sell at $27 million. At one point someone painted it beige and it sold for $20 million. Well, so much for "Ma Vie en Rose". Generally, many of the original houses along this stretch are being developed out of existence and in some instances multiple mega-mansions are being erected on the same lot, sometimes stretching one, two or three rows back from the beach to Gordon Dr. If you see a modest old house from the 1960's or 1970's, the odds are that it won't be there for long before it is sold as a multi-million dollar tear-down and replaced with a mega-mansion, so enjoy these old beach houses while you can.

Naples Pier on a February week day afternoon.

View to the north from the Pier on a February weekday

Naples City Beach looking south toward the Pier from 18th Ave. S

32nd Ave S. and 33rd Ave S. in Port Royal

Parking	🌴
Food, Drink, Amenities	
Toilets/Change Rooms/Showers	🌴
Rentals	
Shelling	🌴 🌴 🌴 🌴
Proximity and variety of off-site amenities	

This section of the beach is the most southerly of the mainland Collier County beach walks and is among my favorites. It is the walk I do most often and since it is just one mile in length, the two mile round-trip makes for a perfect little beach get-away that can be completed in an hour or less. Be warned however, that the walk's magnificent culmination at Gordon Pass, may cause one to linger and the trip can end up taking all day or even an entire lifetime. This is apparently what happened to Roger Gordon who came down here one day in middle of the 19th century, never left and achieved immortality of a sort merely by setting his butt on the sand. If you figure what some people had to go through to achieve immortality (St. Sebastian comes to mind) Roger crushed it.

A surprisingly large number of elements come together in this stretch of beach to make this one of the most interesting walks. First of all, there is very limited public parking in this section of town, as it is one of the most exclusive neighborhoods in all of Florida, aptly named Port Royal. Interestingly, it is not

gated, though if one is thinking nefariously there are video cameras on the utility

poles and in the trees. There are only about 20 public parking spaces between

the two cul de sacs, so the bad news is that you have to get there early (or get

lucky) to get a parking space in season, i.e. between Christmas and Easter. The

good news is that you can bike here easily from just about any place in town. It

is 27 short blocks (most of it on bike lanes along Gulfshore Blvd.) from Naples

famous Fifth Ave. S. shopping district and a mere 15 blocks from the city pier.

Of course, this limiting factor means there are generally very few people on this

beach and in the off-season, rarely any at all.

Port Royal was built in the 1960's as a dredge and fill project in a

mangrove estuary. It would be impossible to develop today because of

environmental regulations. Most of the streets have a salty dog, seafaring

connotation – Rum Row, Gin Lane, Galleon Dr., Spyglass Lane, Cutlass Lane, to

name a few. Depending on your political perspective you can look upon this as

the developers' satirical comment on the nature of the initial buyers as either

pirates or captains of industry and commerce or both. I'll leave that up to you,

but the metaphor works for me either way, present residents included.

Gordon Pass is the main inlet/outlet from the Gulf of Mexico into Naples

Bay. It is also where the Gordon River/Golden Gate Canal confluence of

freshwater enters the Gulf and creates a significant estuary that runs southwards about ten miles as the gull flies toward Marco Island and includes Keewaydin Island, Cannon Island, Little Marco Island and others. Way back in the day before a lot of land development, the watershed for Naples Bay was about 10 square mile while these days it is about 120 square miles and the daily discharge of freshwater into the bay is about 200 million gallons. There is a 20 year plan begun in 2008 to significantly reduce the amount of storm water run-off that reaches Naples Bay and thus increase the salinity of the brackish water to its predevelopment levels and restore its marine fecundity. Oysters and mangroves need a regular tidal flushing of saltwater to thrive. Huge daily doses of strip mall parking lot run-off just don't cut it. In the autumn of 2012, the city officially opened the Golden Gate Canal pumping station which diverts 20 million gallons of freshwater daily from the Gordon River (and thus Naples Bay) into city owned deep wells. That water will be used to supplement fresh water supplies for irrigation.

The spectacular island beaches of Collier County warrant a separate section. This walk offers the first glimpse of Keewaydin Island (once named Key Island) directly opposite and south of Gordon Pass. Technically, Marco Island is said to be the most northerly of the Ten Thousand Islands and one enters them south of Caxambas Pass and Cape Marco or south of Goodland via Coon Key. However, these islands in and around Rookery Bay share many of the same attributes such as large stands of red and black mangroves, limited human habitation and abundant bird and marine life. This came about as a result of various combinations of alliances between governmental and non-governmental environmental agencies that one way or another achieved an end result of hundreds of square miles of undeveloped natural habitat. Both the Rookery Bay National Estuarine Research Reserve and the Conservancy of Southwest Florida are responsible for this wonderful natural resource located smack, dab in the middle of Collier County. The section of the Ten Thousand Islands that is administered by the federal government as the National Wildlife Refuge is 35,000 acres alone but the total area including that which is in Everglades National Park is at least triple that. Most of these islands are small and more suitable for kayaking than walking, but a half-dozen or so provide beach walks that can take one back in time a few hundred years or even a few thousand when one discovers an incongruous high island at 40 or 50 feet above sea level which in all likelihood is an Indian shell mound. Oysters and clams were abundant then and with no limits to harvesting, life was good though keep in mind that there was no mosquito control either. Of course, the chardonnay and horseradish were lacking, but given the size of some of the shell mounds in this general area the Calusa tribe didn't let the lack of Rockefeller recipes or condiments interfere with their pile building program.

As you walk south from 33rd Ave. the dolphins and manatees will be on your right. Those amazing houses on your left are likely owned by people sometimes referred to as the "other half" but more recently as "one percenters". At the end of March 2012 there were three mega-mansions under construction along this section of beach either on in-fill lots or on multi-million dollar teardowns. I don't use the term "mega mansion" lightly. Believe it or not there was a time when a five or ten thousand square foot cottage was enough to mollify most egos. To give you an idea of the magnitude of the wealth reflected here one of those houses is on a lot that sold a few years ago for $18 million (marked down after the real estate crash from $30 million). It will likely serve as a winter residence for a one percent family and they will likely spend a couple of weeks a year here. If they heed the advice of their accountant they'll write off a million dollars in annual interest. By offsetting the taxes they would have paid otherwise over the life of a thirty year term mortgage, the federal government will have paid about half the cost of the lot. One home owner must be on blood thinners as the house appears to have about sixteen fireplaces - in Florida no less. Of course they could be faux flues designed to fake out gawkers and walkers. In case you were going to use your Powerball winnings to buy this particular house, (a) it is not for sale (b) it is assessed at $45M and (c) the local property taxes are just shy of $500,000 a year (deductible of course if you itemize). The most southerly house on this stretch of beach is owned by Pittsburgh native and West Point alumnus, Jack Donahue, the founder of the roughly $400 billion dollar Federated mutual fund empire which is a family business. A number of big wig Republicans (Bush's, Cheney's and Palin's) have been known to lunch at this end of the beach during election year cycles. If you think this estate and grounds are a little much for one family, think again.

He and his wife of sixty plus years, at one point had 13 children, 83 grandchildren, 34 great grandchildren and as far as I know are still counting. The extended family appears to have spilled across Gordon Pass where it is said they own a half dozen or more houses on Keewaydin Island.

It's hard to believe but as you are walking south from 32nd or 33rd it is quite possible to become completely oblivious to all those houses just a few yards away on the left. It kind of depends on what floats your boat. There are a large number of ruined piers that you have to walk around, over or through. There is one derelict pier with about a dozen pilings which has either thirteen cormorants or thirteen pelicans each vying for one of the pilings upon which to sit and this has been going on for at least the 11 years I have lived here and perhaps for generations before. Invariably, there is always one too many birds for the number of pilings resulting in an endless and sometimes very funny game of Musical Chairs to a cacophony of protest as each species reclaims or reaffirms its places on the piles. It is kind of an interesting metaphor for life around the world these days. Even if the only thing you own is a single fish for food and share a 12 inch piling for a home, you must still be prepared to fight for it daily. A true Objectivist would approve. If Atlas did indeed shrug would the cormorant even notice?

About three quarters of the way down the beach, you will encounter a lovely swimming cove with a steel break-water. The cove makes for a neat semi-circular, shallow swimming pool perfect for kids of all ages. The rock break-water offers some good snorkeling along its outer side if the Gulf is calm and periodically various kinds of marine life get stranded in the little tidal pools. There is also some decent snorkeling to be had at the end of the walk along the Gordon Pass jetty and a few partially submerged rock jetties between the cove and the end of the beach. The beach here is windswept, squeaky sand (as you walk lightly run the soles of your bare feet across the surface of the sand) and depending on the wind and tide conditions strewn with shells of all varieties.

Twenty thousand boats are registered in Collier County Florida and while not all of them will transit Gordon Pass for your entertainment, enough of them will. Depending on the time and the day of the week many of the people aboard the excursion boats will wave to you. You can choose to wave back or not. They generally appear to be very happy to have shelled out $50 each for five minutes in Gordon Pass coming and going and perhaps seeing a dolphin or two. I would just ask that you not be too smug about having spent a few quarters in the parking meter (or not), a couple of bucks on this guide book and spending as much time here as suits you. Before you go and start your return journey, look east and up to the most southerly palm tree on Mr. Donahue's estate. From time to time, a Bald Eagle perches here. It is said that the Bald Eagle is a very intelligent bird.

An excursion boat heads out to the Gulf of Mexico in Gordon Pass. The opposite side is the north end of Keewaydin Island. This is as far south as you can get on Naples mainland beaches. From the "Hole in the Hedge" at Doc's Beach House to here is about 17 miles. See the section of the book "Islands without Bridges" to read much more about Keewaydin.

Map Image provided by IslandMapstore.com, Copyright 2011 © Turrell, Hall and Associates

Islands with Bridges – Marco Island

Directions

- Exit #101 South off I75 at Collier Blvd. (County Rd. 951)
- Or follow Route #41 east out of downtown Naples to Collier Blvd.
- Turn right (south) on Collier Blvd. You will be on the island when you cross over the Jolley Bridge

Marco Island is often dubbed as the "The Last Paradise" but the reference is generally misunderstood. It WAS that. It's not that now, but It's still really nice though and worth a couple of visits and some exploration. The moniker refers to the period before its development by the Deltona and Collier corporations in the late 1960's and early 1970's. The reference is to the fact that the developers saw this is as the last paradise in Florida that could be made available for development and in that (at least in this part of the state) they were likely correct. The story of the development of Marco Island parallels the rise of the environmental movement and likely the reason that there are more than ten thousand uninhabited islands immediately to the south of it and no causeway to the Florida Keys. I am extremely grateful to Douglas Waitley author of "The Last Paradise: The Building of Marco Island" for his objective and cogent history of the development of the island and the main reason I am able to comment on it knowledgeably here. Today, while the island still has a huge long crescent shaped beach that is the widest one in the county, actual public access is severely limited. Even one of the best public access spaces in the center of the beach is reserved for residents (of the island not the county) and aptly named, "Residents' Beach" which appears to aggravate hundreds of thousands of visitors annually to no end since parking spaces cannot be purchased even when the residents are not in residence. When Deltona came on the scene in 1962 the main beach called Crescent Beach was deserted and devoid of development, except for a Cold War United States Air Force missile tracking station at Cape Marco that had its only role to play should the US need to launch a missile in the direction of Cuba. Luckily it was never needed, though we came close. As you might recall Cuba was a Soviet satellite in the Caribbean Sea for a generation or two and at one time posed a serious threat as the likely flashpoint for World War Three. Stern diplomacy by the Kennedy Administration ultimately saved the day and made the beaches of Cuba safe for future generations of socialists, communists and Canadians to cavort in discounted comfort.

Barron Collier had owned most of the five and a half mile long island since the 1920's and the company had generally abandoned the idea of developing it after the Great Depression took the wind out of their sails. Ironically, the island as well as one or two to the south were offered to the government of Florida as an environmental preserve in the 1950's for a mere $1.0 million. The government at the time thought the price too steep and demurred. These days that might barely a buy a single condo on the beach or one modest house on a direct access canal. The Colliers even briefly considered a proposal for a gigantic industrial port to process bauxite from Jamaica and oil from Venezuela but nothing came of it and then they came across Deltona and sold it to them for $7.5 million in a buy now, pay later kind of development deal. What happened is fascinating stuff and to quote Paul Harvey I must refer you to Mr. Waitley's 1993 book published by Pineapple Press for the "rest of the story".

As a result of Marco Island's uniqueness as "The Last Paradise" a few more words in general about Florida, development, the environmental movement and capitalist need and greed are appropriate here. I would refer you to two non-fiction books "Everglades: River of Grass" by Marjorie Stoneman Douglas published in 1947 and "The Swamp: The Everglades, Florida and the Politics of Paradise" by Michael Grunwald published 60 years later in 2007. Like book-ends these two brilliant works delineate the evolution of the environmental issue at least as it relates to water. As long as the low lying, wet land was seen as a swamp it appeared wasted (as in the rich soil not being farmed for food), a threat as a source of pestilence (early settlers always drained the swamps first) and an opportunity (as in cheap, fixer upper land for pennies on the dollar). There is an old maxim "Who controls the vocabulary, controls the argument". The publication of Stoneman Douglas' book in the vaunted River of America series (it was the 33rd book published in the 65 book series that spanned decades) changed the dynamic of the discussion. If the Everglades represented moving water albeit slow moving water then as such it was definitely not a swamp. Similarly, salt water swamps also evolved into tidal estuaries as their tide water moved regularly and predictably while generally wetlands underwent a transformation from "wasted land" to threatened habitats of flora and fauna. During this semantic transformation, the federal government in various forms played a large role in the evolution of the environmental vocabulary. John F Kennedy was influenced by Rachel Carson's seminal work "Silent Spring". The Army Corps of Engineers as a result of civil litigation with the developers of Marco Island evolved from jurisdiction over navigable waterways exclusively to jurisdiction over all waters as a direct result. Then in a veritable plethora of environmental activism Congress passed the Environmental Protection Act in 1970; the Clean Water Act in 1972 and in 1973 the Endangered Species Act. All of this while Marco Island was being clear cut of mangroves and dredged and filled to carve out pieces of paradise for middle class Midwesterners.

There can be no doubt that the "need and greed" of speculators of every stripe contributed to the massive public backlash that resulted in the environmental activism of Congress and set the tone for the environmentally aware twenty-first century in which we find ourselves. In the Ten Thousand Islands just south of Marco Island 19th century plume hunters not only decimated the rookeries but murdered the first man charged with the task of protecting the birds from extinction. The price of feathers by weight paid by fashionable milliners in New York exceeded the price of gold. One could argue that while perhaps the movement did not begin here, it certainly achieved a substantive victory here. While the battles rage on there is a defined field of engagement that favors you and me and our access to islands without bridges as well as beaches without barriers.

TIGERTAIL BEACH ON MARCO ISLAND

Directions

- Follow Collier Blvd. in a southerly direction. Go over the new Factory Bay Bridge at the Winn-Dixie (the island's only Supermarket) and watch for the sign for Tigertail which will be on your right.
- Turn right onto Kendall Dr. Follow Kendall to Hernando Dr.
- Turn left at Hernando and proceed west until you reach Tigertail Park in less than a half mile

Parking	🌴🌴🌴🌴
Food, Drink, Amenities	🌴🌴🌴
Toilets/Change Rooms/Showers	🌴🌴🌴🌴🌴
Rentals	🌴🌴🌴🌴
Shelling	🌴🌴🌴🌴🌴
Proximity and variety of off-site amenities	

This is another one of those beaches that most people can't figure out. It is hard to find as you have to pass through a neighborhood to get to the parking lot which while isolated is ample with 210 parking spaces. It too is a Collier County Park with the usual parking fees ($8.00 daily, $50.00 annual, or free local taxpayer window decal pass). Once you park the car and think you're there you aren't even there yet. The real beach still requires a lot of effort to get to. Just like at Clam Pass, thousands of people come here and never make the extra effort to get there. Unlike Clam Pass where a tram takes you the roughly three quarters of a mile to the beach there is no free ride here. You have two choices, either walk a quarter mile across the lagoon in the mangrove muck to the open water or walk about three quarters of a mile south around the lagoon.

If you do this you will have arrived at a living, developing barrier island called Sand Dollar which is just about ten years old (the topography in this area was totally redefined by Hurricane Wilma in 2005) that serves as a refuge and nesting site for a great many shorebirds. Or you can just sit down at the lagoon where the rental chair concession is and fulminate about the fact that this is not really a very nice beach as the mangrove leaf tinted water is brown and smelly and the bottom mucky and tell your friends not to bother with the 20 mile trip from Naples.

If I can convince you to walk around or through the lagoon you will be rewarded. Once you reach the main beach turn right and head north. It is about two miles along the spit to the end of the island. With an exposed northern shore and a sheltered south side lagoon there is much to see here. With northern and westerly winds prevailing during the winter, the sand swept landscape is forever changing and creating naturally sculpted dunes as if nature has run awry with an architect's French curve on the sound side, especially as you approach the mouth of the Marco River to the north and east. As you walk you'll notice that the muddy lagoon at the Tiger Tail parking lot is turning into a turquoise colored sound with the fresh tide water from the east working its way between the two separate beaches. That beach on the south side of the little sound is called Hideaway and we will get to that in the next section. As always, I remain enthralled by the juxtaposition of these curved shapes in white sand with the turquoise waters. The exposed northern side is very interesting as well as it is little visited for obvious reasons and with that northern exposure the shelling is excellent. My nautical charts show an island called Coconut Island that is no longer here. It was wiped out by Hurricane Wilma in 2005 and then subtly, sculpted back into the peninsula that we're walking along. There is excellent shelling and birding on this northern shore and you will pass a number of restricted nesting areas for terns and plovers. Please be respectful of these and keep your distance and do bear in mind that this area is constantly in flux and will likely be different from what I saw when you get here.

The view of the lagoon at Tigertail Beach The high rises in the background are on Cape Marco.

Tigertail Park picnic area and concession stand. You can buy a cold beer here, as long as you consume it on the deck.

Coconut Point, for want of a better name is about a mile walk from Tigertail Beach, which is the only land access to this spot. Hideaway Beach lagoon is to the right where the damp sand is showing.

Hideaway Beach is across the lagoon. This view is from the spot of the previous photograph but looking south. The boat is Gunkhole Gertie, aka Gertie. More Gertie and Bernie adventures can be seen at my weblog, REACHYOURPERFECTBEACH.BLOGSPOT.COM

HIDEAWAY BEACH ON MARCO ISLAND

Directions

- Follow Collier Blvd. in a southerly direction. Go over the new Factory Bay Bridge at the Winn-Dixie (the island's only Supermarket) and watch for the sign for Tigertail which will be on your right.
- Turn right onto Kendall Dr. At the end of Kendall Dr. you will reach the neighborhood Gate House. Good luck talking your way inside, but having a friend or relative that lives here will improve your chances dramatically.

This beach lives up to its name and is indeed hidden away and you can't get there without a challenging swim or a difficult wet and muddy walk that is about a mile long. Walking in the mangrove muck is hard, physical work and not at all like walking on the beach, so a mile in the mud is more like three on the beach. I once found myself in mud up to my chest down in the Keys. If you haven't experienced it yourself take my word for it and don't bother. If you have taken the long walk from Tiger Tail on the outside as outlined above, then you will see this beach to the immediate south and it is tantalizingly close, though depending on the tide table I wouldn't recommend the swim as being worth the risk or the trouble. Unlike the Clam Pass/Pelican Beach walk-over, this is a definite swim-over. Road access is impossible for most people as Hideaway Beach is located inside a residential development of multi-million dollar homes that has 24/7 gated security. I wouldn't fret about it, as the beach merely parallels the sound and is not on open water. It is annoying that though this beach is ostensibly public and is re-nourished periodically with public funds, the public has no realistic way in, other than by boat of course. Having been to the beach clubhouse once for a business lunch, I see no particular reason why you need to be put out by the lack of public access but you would certainly be within your rights to wonder why tax dollars are being used to replenish this particular beach when Mother Nature has made it clear on a repeated basis that she is quite capable of giving and taking sand as she sees fit and redistributing much of it back out to Coconut Point. At some point she'll likely blow another cut into the sand spit and we'll have Coconut Island all over again. I'd look forward to exploring that with you in future editions of this book. This has already happened in the area just a mile southeast of Cape Romano where Hurricane Wilma made landfall and took a big sandbar island on the Cape Romano shoals out. The new island is dubbed locally as "Second Chance Island" and has become a rookery for the threatened sea bird known as the least tern.

SOUTH BEACH ON MARCO ISLAND

Directions

- Follow Collier Blvd. past the Marriott and past the Hilton as far south as you can go before the road turns sharply left.
- Watch for the signs just before Cape Marco. Parking is on the left and the public beach access is on the right

Parking	🌴
Food, Drink, Amenities	🌴 🌴 🌴
Toilets/Change Rooms/Showers	🌴 🌴
Rentals	🌴 🌴 🌴 🌴
Shelling	🌴 🌴
Proximity and variety of off-site amenities	🌴 🌴 🌴

This is Crescent Beach, the spectacular beach that awed the Mackle brothers (principals of the Deltona Corporation) and arguably led to the ultimate demise of Deltona. A pre-development aerial photograph which can easily be found on Google Images, clearly demonstrates how the "wow factor" might have influenced the Mackle brothers and Collier family to try and profit from this amazing jewel in the rough. From Cape Marco north to the point where the Tiger Tail lagoon begins is about 2 ½ miles. At its widest point it is about 1,000 feet of sand and more often than not averages about 500 feet. It is easily the biggest beach in the county. The public access parking lot has only 70 parking spaces, so if you want to visit, get here early. People do park illegally in the culverts on the side streets near the public access, but whether or not you get ticketed is entirely hit or miss.

You might think that with such a huge beach and such limited parking you and a handful of your closest friends could have this beach pretty much to yourselves and you might be right much of the time. Along the entire eastern edge of the beach there is a long curving line of very tall buildings some as high as eighteen floors and these buildings do hold a lot of people at certain times of the year, roughly from Thanksgiving to Easter. There are about a half dozen or so big hotels and timeshare resorts along this stretch that at their peak occupancy will account for at least 5,000 people or more all of whom are there for the same reason you are. In addition there are three dozen or more substantial condominium buildings that will house double that number again and that's not even mentioning the roughly 3,000 single family homes and hundreds of low rise condo's east of the beach, many of the occupants of which can walk to Crescent Beach. To give you an idea of how densely developed this stretch of beach is, consider that when the local community does its Easter Sunrise service they have a hard time finding a place to set up where the people can actually see the sun to the east without having to wait until noon. For your information they use a little sliver of space between the Marriott and the 18 story Madeira condominium tower.

When you step on Crescent Beach from the South Beach public access, to your left is Cape Marco, the site of the old missile tracking station. There are six luxury condominium high rise buildings on this one 30 acre site alone named in no particular order: Belize, Veracruz, Tampico, Cozumel, Monterrey and Merida. With resale prices averaging between $500 and $1,000 per sq. foot of living space depending on the floor and the building, any single ONE of these condos nowadays is worth more than the entire island was worth roughly sixty years ago. It is fair to say that the Mackle family was right in its appraisal that this was and still is a very coveted place in the sun that people would aspire to be a part of. If you could see anything south of Cape Marco (unfortunately unless you own one of these units these days you can't) you would see on the other side of Caxambas Pass a series of islands with a long run of beaches called Dickman's, Kice, Morgan and Cape Romano which have been the subject of some of my blogs and present some of my favorite places to boat and kayak. These islands figure prominently in the final chapter of this book as well as in my weblog called REACHYOURPERFECTBEACH.BLOGSPOT.COM.

When you go north from the public access you have two miles of broad beach in view and a couple of big hotels like the Hilton and the Marriott that you can have lunch or cocktails at if you are so inclined. The old Radisson hotel was recently converted to Marriott timeshares. The sand on this beach at this time was dredged here in 1991 which provides an interesting reminder to us all that beaches are indeed living things and they come and go as nature, not mankind decrees. All of the "original" sand that the Mackles' saw in the 1960's

had eroded away during the prior thirty years of development. When you are

directly in front of the Marriott, it is notable that this may be the only beach that

you will ever walk on, where there is a reasonable chance that there could be

Spanish treasure or pirate gold under your feet. Florida such as it was defined

at the time was administered by the Spanish out of Havana for about 300 years

and it's not as if sunken Spanish ships are a rarity. Hundreds of them are known

to have sunk for one reason or another including the great Hurricane of 1715

and this exact spot is a mere 200 miles from Havana or less than a 2 day sail at

the time give or take a few days to dodge the Keys and the reefs. Florida was

used as a giant ranch and the huge feral hogs the size of "L'il Sebastian" that

run wild in the uplands around here to this day are a continuing testament to

that. When The Marco Beach Hotel (it and the prime real estate under it was

ultimately sold to Mass Mutual Insurance who have Marriott run their hotel now)

was under construction, an engineer was doing a little moonlighting on

company time with company equipment when he turned up evidence of metal

buried deep in the sand. In addition, what appeared to be wood from a ship

came up in the drillings as well. The developer put a stop to the moonlighting

even though it appeared that a Spanish treasure map the engineer was

referencing showed a crescent shaped beach and a shoreline that bore a

striking resemblance to the exact place they had just found old oak, way down

deep in an area where oak never grows. To get to the bottom of the mystery the developer likely would have had to delay construction of the hotel and invest a considerable amount of money in equipment for pumps, pipes and shorings. Of course, they might also have discovered archeological antiquities i.e. ships' cannon for example, which might have closed down their main construction project for years and they had bigger fish to fry or so they concluded. They chose to close up the hole and leave the mystery unsolved and it's all still there out there. Sounds like a great reality TV series and publicity stunt just waiting for the right people to put it all together don't you think? The Curse of Oak Island is a big hit for the History Channel just now and it has me very interested. Besides you could dig in the warm sunshine on a sandy beach 365 days a year instead of a cold, muddy swamp for 90 days.

Cape Marco is as far south as you can walk on the beach in Marco Island. The shuttered balconies usually indicate the owners are not in residence. On the opposite side of these buildings is Kice Island.

Somewhere under these Marco Marriott Chickee Huts lays buried a Spanish Treasure. Just a reminder if you missed that part. "Not all Tiki's are Chickee's but all Chickee's are Tiki's".

Crescent Beach on Marco Island with a view to the north from Cape Marco.

It is possible at times to find a reasonably priced parking spot across Collier Blvd. from the Marriott Hotel. Tell the attendant you are going to lunch here and then do a little beaching, or vice versa.

Restaurants near Marco Island Beaches

- Capri Fish House; 4.0 out of 5.0 on Trip Advisor; dine inside or outside; waterfront; bay view; on the Isles of Capri, last right before the Jolley Bridge $$$

- Sunset Grille; 3.5 out of 5.0 on Trip Advisor; dine inside or outside; waterfront; gulf view; in the Apollo Condominium Building adjacent to the South Beach access walkway; $$$

- Quinn's on the Beach; 4.0 out of 5.0 on Trip Advisor; dine inside or outside; waterfront; gulf view; in the Marco Marriott Resort; access from the hotel or the beach directly; $$$$

- Nene's Kitchen; 4.5 out of 5.0 on Trip Advisor; dine inside or outside; no view; located on Collier Blvd. just south of Kendall which is the turn to Tigertail and Hideaway Beaches; $$

- Michelbob's Ribs; 4.5 out of 5.0 on Trip Advisor; take out only; open from 5:00 to 8:00 and on the right side of the Blvd. as you leave any Marco Island Beach; $$$

- Cocomo's Grill; 4.0 out of 5.0 on Trip Advisor; dine inside; no view; next to Michelbob's and on the right side of the Blvd. as you leave any Marco Island Beach; $$$

- Beach Club Bar and Grill; 4.0 out of 5.0 on Trip Advisor; dine poolside or fireside; Tiki Bar; on the grounds of the Hilton Resort south of Quinn's and north of Sunset Grille;$$$

- Paradise Café; 4.0 out of 5.0 on Trip Advisor; dine inside or outside; waterfront; gulf view; also on the grounds of the Hilton Resort;$$$

Islands without Bridges (North of Marco) - Keewaydin

Parking	🌴 🌴
Food, Drink, Amenities	
Toilets/Change Rooms/Showers	🌴 🌴
Rentals	
Shelling	🌴 🌴 🌴 🌴 🌴
Proximity and variety of off-site amenities	

The most exciting thing about this island is that it is so boring. Hardly anyone lives here and except for holiday week-ends and one big party week-end at the end of May at the far southern extremity relatively few people come here. While there are 50 platted private lots on the 8 mile long island, (six of them are owned by Donohue's) many of them have never been developed and those few that have been are for the most part unobtrusive. Recently a member of Vice President Joe Biden's family bought a house in the south end of the island. In addition, a number of lots were purchased by various conservation agencies and much of the island falls within the Rookery Bay National Estuarine Reserve which controls development rights over 110,000 acres in this general area. Much of the land is not suitable for development as the lagoons and bays on the east side that we use to access the island beach on blustery days, are quite tight up against the beach, leaving little room for a building and no space at all for septic fields.

Known at one time as Key Island, the name was changed by the operators of a series of "Outward Bound" type sleep away camps called Keewaydin Camps to reference the Onondaga name for the "Northwest Wind" character contained in the famous Henry Wadsworth Longfellow poem entitled the "Song of Hiawatha". These camps, fourteen in all at their zenith were located in Vermont, Maine and Ontario among other places. One of them, founded in 1893 appears still to be operating in northern Ontario at Lake Temagami. As I was researching their website I was surprised to find that it is located just 100 miles by bush plane from where I earned my Boy Scout canoeist merit badge in Algonquin Park more than fifty years ago. That episode evokes a fond but painful memory in that I had to carry a canoe that weighed much more than me for a 100 yard portage connecting Smoke Lake to Grape Lake without putting it down. I not only whittled my own paddle from a piece of redwood, but with the rest of the troop we shaped the canoe from fiberglass matte and resin, on a group owned mould. With the canoe on my aching shoulders it soon became apparent that we had used way too much fiberglass and ought to have spent another day or two sanding it away. When the Keewaydin Camp on Key Island closed as a result of financial difficulties traced back to the Camp Director and his spouse's misallocation of funds, the facility was converted to a lodge. It was listed on the National Register of Historic Places in 1987, closed in 1999 and is now privately owned.

Despite its apparent seclusion, depending on wind and tides, this island is readily accessed from various embarkation points in the Naples area. If you or a friend has a boat with a motor, you can be there in minutes. By paddle it is generally less than a one hour trip with a favorable tide to three different landing areas. From the east you can use the free Shell Island launch and follow the Hall Bay navigation markers west to the intersection of the Intracoastal, cross over it and at Green marker 28A, enter the channel between Little Marco Island and Cannon Island. The white beach straight ahead is your destination, though it is the smaller beach on the east or channel side of Keewaydin and not the mind bogglingly huge beach on the west side that everyone raves about. You can beach your craft here and walk across the marked trail a few yards to get to the big beach. On this stretch you were travelling between Little Marco Island on your right and Cannon Island on the left. After Little Marco ends in a long mudflat, if you want to cruise down the left side before you cross the channel to the big island, there is a long narrow beach interrupted by large Casuarina root balls that is certainly one of the prettiest sights around. There are a lot of variable currents in this area known locally as Hurricane Pass and Cannon Island turns itself into Sea Oat Island in this general area, which is constantly changing. The small bays bordered by the stumps face west to Keewaydin and I have spent quite a few glorious hours on this little stretch watching the big boys with their motorized toys across the channel. You can also access this area from the south by renting kayaks at the Isle of Capri or renting a motorboat or pontoon boat from the Marco River Marina. If you feel

more comfortable with a commercial day trip, there are plenty of those around

including the big catamaran at Naples City Dock called "Sweet Liberty" that

offers shelling cruises for a very reasonable price and numerous smaller

operators of pontoon boats. Though it is the shortest route, I don't recommend

coming to Keewaydin Island's west side through Gordon Pass when embarking

from the north but it is very easy to do when conditions are favorable. If you are

car topping, you can park at the fore-mentioned 33rd Ave. South cul de sac

and paddle south a little more than a mile and you will be there. However, this

generally works only when there is no wind or the forecast is for very slight winds.

Wind speeds of over 10 knots, from any direction other than east will usually kick

up two or three foot waves. Though I have done it my little 8 foot kayak,

crossing Gordon Pass between and among very large boat wakes, tidal currents

and incoming surf make for a tricky crossing that is not for the faint of heart but

on that particular day it culminated in a magnificent day on the beach for me.

When approaching from the north in pretty much any weather, it is preferable

to launch from Bayview Park's boat ramp where Keewaydin is a clearly visible

hop and a skip to the west. The kicker though is that you still have to find a

good public landing spot on the island that is not choked with impenetrable red

mangroves. If you coast with an outgoing tide to the Intracoastal markers and

turn left (south) then Keewaydin will be on your right and you will be in Dollar

Bay. About a mile and a half into this segment look for Green Marker 67 and

Red Marker 66 and then paddle southwest to find the pass into the mangroves. You won't see it when you start out but it will reveal itself as you get closer. It is an entrance to a series of mangrove channels that culminates at Bartell Bay in the south and will take you to either of two different landing sites, about a mile from the north end of the island. The bays that you enter out of the mangrove channel literally back up to the big beach. The mangrove channels are not easy to navigate without a guide the first time and while technically you can't get lost in here as there is only one way in and out, there are a lot of dead-ends and you feel like you could, especially if you can't discern the opening for the way out. There is a Google Earth Graphic of this route on my blog, if a picture is more than these words to you. Don't try this one on your own, until you get a chance to study the area and make a few other practice runs. If you have a GPS with a chart plotter you can get in and out of here quite readily with just three or four waypoints. It's also recommended that before attempting this trip you ought to study the area on Google Maps and bring a paper chart in case your GPS runs out of battery power. There are two crossovers to the main beach about 500 yards apart from this coastal lagoon known as Bartell Bay. They are hard to miss in that there is an obvious break in the vegetation when they come into view. The first one comes up rather abruptly in the right after a half mile long run in a relatively wide straight channel.

Another route that will give you access to the center of the island which is also its most remote point, is to look for Red Marker 46 on the Intracoastal. This part of the beach is so isolated, that it is recommended as a camping site by the Naples Kayak Company and from time to time you may encounter some fellow free spirits here. If you are coming from either the north or south by motorized craft, just follow the numbers. For my purposes, it is too long and too busy to follow the channel to this mark from either end. I recommend you take an outgoing tide from the Shell Island launch site and paddle north through Rookery Bay. It is only a couple of miles long so a two knot favorable tidal current coupled with a few hundred well placed paddle strokes in a northwesterly direction will suffice to get you there in less than a hour. The bay is very shallow with a mean water depth of less than three feet, so there is very little boat traffic. A pod of four dolphins once cavorted with me in here for a delightful half hour. At the north end of the bay, the channel takes you out to the Intracoastal again with Holloway Island on your left. Green Marker 47 is visible first and when you turn the corner in a southerly direction, you'll see the Red Marker 46. Opposite it, there is a shell beach landing area that you can use to beach your boat but it is not ideal as the channel is narrow here and the wake from boats passing at high speeds is sure to mess up whatever mooring or anchoring scheme you have managed to contrive. The path to the big beach is about 30 yards long and depending on how long you are planning to stay, you might wish to carry your kayak across so your gear is not out of sight as you are wandering up and down the main beach. You have roughly 4 miles of beach in both directions before it ends so this is likely as close as most of us are even going to get to gazing at a long stretch of uninterrupted white beach sand as far as we can see in either direction.

Keewaydin Island's unusually long, uninterrupted and unlit beach makes it prime real estate for nesting sea turtles. According to Rookery Bay research, during a fourteen year period from 1994 to 2007 more than 134,000 sea turtles were hatched here. Unfortunately in the summer of 2012 the tidal surge from Hurricane Isaac which never even made landfall in Florida is said to have wiped out more than 200 sea turtle nests on this one island alone. With each nest containing up to 100 eggs, that had the potential to be a better than average year. Perhaps as many 15,000 to 20,000 of the cute little critters never got to punch their one in a thousand tickets for their shot at the world cruise. Of the seven species of sea turtles in the entire world, five are found in Florida and three of these nest along the Gulf Coast. These are the loggerhead, green and leatherback. About 61,000 loggerheads nest throughout Florida on both coasts, about 6,000 greens and only 700 leatherbacks. If you would like to learn more about sea turtles there is an informative documentary entitled "Turtle: The Incredible Journey" that is available from Amazon. I was astonished by the hand that they were dealt by nature and the travails over which they triumph during their Homeric odyssey. Of all the places where they might have settled, from the Azores to the Caribbean - like Ulysses they choose to come home again to Keewaydin Island. That says it all about this place.

Let me know if you spot anyone. The ATV tracks likely belong to the the CCSO (Collier County Sheriff's Office) searching in vain for wanton lawbreakers. They could also have been made by the Turtle Patrol which travels up and down the beach daily in nesting season. This beach alone had just under 300 nests in 2014. All of Collier's beaches had more than 1,300. Two of the world's best government jobs are both to be had here on just one little island.

Approaching the North end of Keewaydin Island, its most densely developed area. The rocky point of Gordon Pass is visible in the upper left corner.

Sea Turtle crawl. There are almost 2X as many "False Crawls" as real nests on this island. The inbound and outbound flipper marks are clearly visible.

The northern most point on Keewaydin Island. Marker 000 is their own island marker system. The Donahue homestead is across the channel

Islands Without Bridges – (South of Marco) – Kice, Dickman's, Morgan's Island, Cape Romano Island, Coon Key, Panther Key, Whitehorse Key, Brush Key, Jackfish Key, and more

Parking	🌴🌴🌴🌴
Food, Drink, Amenities	🌴🌴🌴
Toilets/Change Rooms/Showers	🌴🌴🌴
Rentals	
Shelling	🌴🌴🌴🌴🌴
Proximity and variety of off-site amenities	🌴🌴

It was difficult to decide what islands to include in this section and what to call them. First of all, they keep changing and the bigger islands keep breaking apart, like icebergs. The table above represents amenities at the boat launch ramps and obviously not at the beaches themselves. All of these beaches are rustic and in their natural state. Google Earth currently identifies nine distinct named land masses in the five mile run of beach just south of Cape Marco but for our purposes three will do nicely. These are named Dickman's, Kice and Cape Romano islands. The former didn't exist back in 1974 (it was merely Dickman's Point on Kice Island) when the developers of Marco Island were forced to cede Kice Island to conservation as wetlands mitigation for dredge and fill permits that they were granted on Marco Island. If not for this, there would likely have been a bridge from Cape Marco to Kice and another five mile stretch of high rise condo towers to rival the strand on Marco Island. As it is, this area presents a rare opportunity to see what the area looked like 500 or even 1,000 years ago, when the Calusa tribe ran the region.

As of December 2013 during my last trip down to Cape Romano from Caxambas boat ramp, things had changed dramatically from just a couple of years earlier when we took an Irwin 28 sailboat down the length of the coast to the Cape. Hurricane Wilma made landfall here in October of 2005 and dramatically changed things, so that is the mostly likely reason that things are not as they appear on the official nautical chart. All of my trips to Cape Romano, about a half dozen in all, took place after Wilma, but observable changes likely due to storms though some admittedly due to tide cycles, made each subsequent trip one of discovery. For example, on the first trip with the Irwin we anchored offshore and my son and I swam to the beach. We had to cross ten or twenty yards of sand to get to the famous dome houses. If you haven't seen these, take a moment now to do a Google Image search and check them out or check out my blogs or YouTube videos. There is nothing else like it in the world. By the way, this is one of those places where swimming is not recommended as the tidal currents between the Cape and the infamous Cape Romano shoals can be a real challenge. On my swim to shore, I grabbed hold of the anchor line and the force of the current pulled my shorts off and sent them on a journey 90 miles south to Marathon. I guess it was a good thing I had lost a couple of inches of waist size and was no longer in them. During a trip n

2012 my son and I paddled our kayak under the pilings of these same dome houses. In the 2013 video I've posted on YouTube, my daughter and I took Gunkhole Gertie right up to the ruins. At the north end, what was once Dickman's Point on the nautical chart is now an island separated from the larger Kice Island by a new, rambunctious Pass without a name, but I think it would be safe to call it Dickman's Pass. This is a neat little pass for a fast swim, float or kayak ride on an incoming tide. There can even be a little white water if your timing is good. Don't try it on an outbound tide as there is no telling where you will end up. The south end of Kice Island still ends at Blind Pass, but I found the beach blocked by stumps and trees just north of Blind Pass. When travelling south from Blind Pass down the western side, we entered a recently minted pass about two thirds of the way down that gave access to Morgan Bay, so I guess we can call that one New Morgan Pass. At Morgan Bay, you can re-enter the beach at any of a half dozen random cuts. The old Morgan Pass at the southern end of the island as identified on the nautical chart is no longer there. By now you get the drift, so let's go back to the top and start with how to get to the most interesting beaches, from where to embark, and what to look for when you get there though its beginning to look like this section might need frequent updates. It's a good thing we are doing an e-book.

The preferred launch site for this area is Caxambas Boat Ramp operated by Collier County Parks and Recreation though we've made the trip from the Goodland Boat Ramp, south and east of here as well. This latter route is very exposed to south winds and breakers and requires a longer trip in more open water, but certainly doable under the right conditions. To get to Caxambas Boat Ramp, take Collier Blvd. south on Marco, proceed past the fore mentioned South Beach parking lot and around the turn at Cape Marco to where the road ends. The entrance to the large parking lot is on the right. There are decent bathrooms here as well as a marina store that sells live bait, charts, snacks and supplies. There is no overnight parking available here, so if you wish to stay out camping or in your boat on any of these beaches, you will have to launch from Goodland, where for an additional $10.00 per night fee, you can safely park your car and trailer. My daughter and I camped at Blind Pass in October of 2014 on our whale bone search. From the ramp it is a very short paddle of less than half an hour west to Dickman's Pass. If this is the first trip down here for you, I'd recommend you do Dickman's Pass and the beach on Dickman's Island as the first destination. You will never be out of sight of Cape Marco's high rise condominiums to reassure you and it is a short and easy trip back. There are usually a few porpoises in this area. As you become more familiar with the area you can expand your range for Blind Pass about a one hour paddle south along a marked navigation channel with a favorable outgoing tide and there are a few alternative paddle trails to and from it. As your crowning achievement, lastly try Cape Romano and Morgan Bay via the inside passage down the Morgan River. The Morgan River runs south out of the big bay at the eastern entry to Blind Pass Channel. You can't miss it. The latter will likely take the better part of two hours and do take note of the tides and wind to make your life a little easier. Surprisingly a strong wind from the east which has a calming effect on the outer coast for which we are always headed, makes for quite a roller coaster ride down Blind Pass Channel in a small craft. The rollers ride right through the one and a quarter mile long channel which runs due west. Of course, if you have an east wind or a calm day without any breakers you can make the whole trip down the exposed west side. You can see an example of Gunkhole Gertie's run down the outside of Kice Island in October of 2014 on my blog. Keep in mind that the weather is variable and just because you got down there, doesn't mean it is going to let you come back the same way. It would be better to learn the inside passage routes first, so that you can fall back on them to work your way back to the ramp at Caxambas.

As with many of the beaches in this area, there is a downside. Large hotels on Marco Island and tour groups including jet-ski flotillas and shelling cruises use these passages a lot in season. Just when you thought you were in the middle of a wilderness created exclusively for your enjoyment, you might find yourself in the middle of a group of jet skiers each of whom have paid someone $175 to be where you are. They usually don't stay long and are off to the next place before they become a serious bother, but it is as annoying as finding a nest of ants or a swarm of wasps at your perfect picnic. However, they too will have earned the bragging rights to have seen everything that I have seen over a decade, in two very brief hours. The small shelling cruise catamarans stay a little longer, but there are usually only a handful of people on them and the joy emanating from their sense of place as evidenced by their broad smiles, shouts and squeals of delight at their discoveries generally allows me to forgive them their encroachments. Every now and again, just as you think yourself totally alone in the universe in a tightly woven mangrove tunnel, seemingly miles from anywhere or anyone you will come across a flats boat fishing charter captain with a couple of guys on board who have paid hundreds of dollars to be in your particular neck of the woods today. The irony of it all, is that if you had the height and the perspective you could see Cape Marco and all of those multi-million condo towers, always just a couple of miles to the north.

You'll need to pick your spots along this five mile long multi-island stretch of beach as natural obstacles make walking the entire length impossible. For example, as an introduction you could walk south along what was once Dickman's Point. Additionally, you can walk north from the right side of Dickman's Pass and as this whole stretch is just a half mile long, sooner or later you will put the pieces together and you've walked your first island beach from tip to toe. Kice Island is similar though on my last two visits the north end of the beach was impassable with stumps within a few yards south of Dickman's Pass and I couldn't get more than two thirds of a mile north on the beach with my approach from Blind Pass. The same can be said for Cape Romano Island generally (called Big Morgan Island on the west side of the Morgan River) and there are a great many more water interruptions there. Cape Romano Island also has a beach that runs the entire length of the south and east sides that is ideally suited for gunkholing as there are lots of dead trees with shell hash in the roots, ruins of failed buildings and camps and even a canal to nowhere where there is a wrecked boat stuck in the mangrove mud. While the beach may be good for gunkholing, swimming here is not recommended as the channel drops off to depth steeply and the tidal currents are swift as a result of the large volume of water squeezed between the expansive Cape Romano shoals and the island. In the shape of an irregular circle, these shoals measure more than 18 miles in circumference. Many of the keys in this region, including Helen Key east of Cape Romano have large sandy landing areas that would pass for a really neat beach in other parts of the world and are just nameless non-descript deposits of shells and sand here. If you need a Plan B, as I sometimes do, go to any spot on a beach that appeals to you on any one of these islands without bridges, plunk your butt down in the sand and eat, drink, read, fish, swim, float or tan and then call it a great day with your return paddle. Enjoy your perfect moment on the perfect beach wherever it is, as you may never pass this way again and even if you do it's likely that it will be different.

The beaches in the rest of the Ten Thousand Islands are made more from shells than sand, are generally short but sweet, are much more rustic than what you might be used to and are often stunning in their beauty. They can be bug infested at dawn and evenings year round with biting midges known colloquially as "no-see-ums". Mosquito season is generally said to last from May to October, so lounging around to catch rays on bare skin is not a highly desirable activity in this particular neck of the woods. Those beach landings that are inside of Everglades National Park (but still part of Collier County), such as Tiger Key, Picnic Key, Jewel Key or Rabbit Key require a lot of planning and the payment of a nightly fee. Those that are north of the Park boundaries and part of the Ten Thousand Island National Wildlife Refuge such as Whitehorse Key, Hog Key, Brush Key, Jackfish Key and Panther Key require neither. Not all of them require overnight stays as many are reachable by day trippers with a small outboard. Most of them are too remote to paddle to and from in daylight hours, except perhaps for Coon Key, Helen's Key and Brush Key.

For my closing words to this second edition of this far from perfect or ever finished book, I refer you back to the subtitle which evolved during the promotion of the first edition that was published in 2012. It reads "Everything you didn't know you wanted to know about Collier County Florida's 35 miles of beaches". So for your last little known fact, please be aware that there are more than Ten Thousand Islands in the eponymous wilderness refuge. No-one really knows how many there are, and the federal government rightfully does not want to have to change the name every couple of years at great expense to the "Eleven Thousand Islands National Wildlife Refuge" and so on. Some say there are likely more than 14,000 and some say there are many fewer. However here is a little anecdote that clearly demonstrates the numbering conundrum. Within the past few years Jackfish Key was two islands separated by a very shallow channel. Recently shell matter began to build up on the south side of the little channel and has connected the two islands with a nice south facing beach landing. On the north side, the former channel functions like a canal, leading to a lagoon at the back of the beach that can also be used to land small craft. So the two islands have become one. At about the same time, I was standing on a substantial and relatively large island of a few acres that I could not find on an aerial photograph. Unless, I was badly lost or crazy, something had to explain it. There was a position co-ordinate given for a mudflat in the area on the aerial and when I used my handheld GPS to get my present location, it matched those co-ordinates exactly. That in essence is the saga of the island beaches and why this project represents another "Never Ending Story". The two keys at Jackfish became one and the one that wasn't one became one and the net effect on the island count was exactly zero. In a few hundred or a few thousand years those shell landings may be battered and washed and windswept until the shells become sand and then someone will once again reach their perfect beach.

A nameless island among ten thousand

Author posing as paleontologist on Kice Island with a whale skull

PHOTO CREDIT: LAUREN RATH

Author at Blind Pass during the summer of 2012

The author just north of Blind Pass on Kice Island, appearing to flaunt his paddling pectorals in a new shirt. PHOTO CREDIT: ANDREW RATH

Gunkhole Gertie at Panther Key. The blog about this adventure can be found by googling the first part of this caption.

Just east of Sea Oat Island and a surprisingly short paddle from the Capri Fish House this place is literally catty corner from Coconut Point on Marco Island

I bid you adieu! Google Kice Island Skull for this adventure

Made in United States
Orlando, FL
13 April 2022

16800448R00091